Treat *King* Him Like a

Nikk,
Praise the Lord!
I love you. I pray
this book bless you.
I equip you to treat Cheap
like a King!

Love me some
you! [signature]

Treat *King* Him Like a

Sheila D. Poole

Hunter Heart Publishing
DuPont, Washington

Treat Him Like a King
Copyright © 2011 Sheila D. Poole

First Edition: November 2011

Please note that the name satan and related names are not capitalized. We choose not to acknowledge him, even to the point of violating grammatical rules.

To order products, or for any other correspondence:

Hunter Heart Publishing
P.O. Box 354
DuPont, Washington 98327
Tel. (253) 906-2160 – Fax: (253) 912-1667
E-mail: publisher@hunterheartpublishing.com
Or reach us on the internet: www.hunterheartpublishing.com

"Offering God's Heart to a Dying World"

This book and all other Hunter Heart Publishing™ books are available at Christian bookstores and distributors worldwide.

Chief Editor: Brenda Mates

Creative design: Odette Hannah
Cover format and logos: Exousia Marketing Group www.exousiamg.com

ISBN: 978-1-937741-93-8

For Worldwide Distribution, Printed in the United States of America.

Dedication

This book is dedicated to my king, my boo, Robert J. Poole, Jr. You know I'm loving me some you! You love me so good; you love me so right; from the crown of my head to the soles of my size six feet. Other than Jesus, you are the best thing that has ever happened to me since the *Whatchamacallit* hit the candy store in the 70's! Always and forever, it's you and me baby. You are truly a gift from God!

Acknowledgments

First and foremost how could I not acknowledge the Lord! God You have been so good to me and Your grace has been sufficient. Thank You for enabling me to write about what You have taught me. Your unfailing love never ceases to amaze me.

Joshua and Shekinah, you are a source of great joy in my life! You are a constant reminder to me that my Redeemer lives! Your lives are a testimony to the glory of God. I love you! Always Rep da King!

Apostle Nate and Pastor Valerie Holcomb, the connection has made the difference. IAAH! Your leadership has made a profound impact on my life and I am forever grateful.

Much love and thanks goes out to Deborah Hunter and Hunter Heart Publishing. Your gift has freed me to flow in my gift! Thank You! You're a jewel to the Body of Christ.

Odette Hannah, the cover artwork is the bomb.com! Thank you for your love, creativity and support on this project.

Danielle (Dani) Belgrave, thank you for so willingly editing and proofreading this book. Your insights and attention to detail really helped in making this project excellent.

Veronica Brown, who knew your words would bring this book out of me! Oh yeah, God did! He's the one that dropped it on you! Thanks for allowing Him to use you as a catalyst in my life.

Dr. Luke and LaLaura, you know who you are! Your relationship and friendship have inspired me in more ways than one. I've watched how you honor each other. Your marriage truly glorifies the Father.

Destiny Christian Center, thanks for all your love, prayers and support. I'm honored to co-labor with you in the kingdom.

Dad and Mom, it would be remiss of me not to take this moment to honor you. Thanks for supporting everything I do! Love you!

Foreword

Marriage is not what is depicted in fictitious literature, love songs, or movies—you don't fall in love and live happily ever after. It takes God the Father, the Son, the Holy Spirit, and a lot of hard work. Along with a little give-and-take, it requires knowledge, wisdom, and a willingness to labor in order to make a good, strong, and secure marriage.

In Pastor Sheila Poole's book, *Treat Him Like a King*, she has travailed and given birth to many truths about marriage. Because of her life experiences, Sheila knows that God can transform two lives and make them one. Since she opened the Book and found the place where it was written of her, she became transparent so that God could use her to help others through this powerful work.

According to Isaiah 1:17, "Learn to do well…" Allow the Holy Spirit to breathe on and teach you how to treat your husband like a king. From beginning to end, I believe you will learn to redeem some things, strengthen some things, and avoid some things. Pastor Sheila reveals that it is never too late, and that God has the answer, the blueprint, the pattern, and the plan for every marriage.

If marriage is not done God's way, it is out of God's will. Not only does Pastor Sheila live God's way, she has the Kingdom perspective and mindset on marriage. She allows the King of Kings to reign and rule and out of her womb has come: *Treat Him Like a King.*

Pastor Valerie Holcomb
Christian House of Prayer, Killeen, TX

Table of Contents

Introduction

As I reflect back over my marriage and how God brought it all together, I can sum it all up in three words, I'm just grateful. Many of you reading this may have already read my first book entitled, *He Redeemed My Time*. It's my life story, and I will sum it up for you. I first tried sex at 11, had sex for the first time at 13, was sexually active throughout high school, sexually abused in college and had "the wanna be married blues" most of my saved, single life. Nevertheless, in spite of me, God saw to it that I had no children before I got married, healed me of a sexually transmitted disease before I knew Him, saved me from hell at the age of 19, reconnected me with my best friend and for the past 19 years we have been happily married. It shouldn't be so. That's why I'm just grateful.

It's been a wonderful life being married and I love it! Robert and I have grown together over the years as we have purposed to love God. It keeps getting sweeter and sweeter, and sometimes I'm left scratching my head feeling like I am living out a fairy tale. Now, don't get me wrong, we have had our challenges, but I'm grateful that he's the one I have challenges with and not one of those Joe's from my past. Shouldn't this be the testimony of all Christian marriages? I think so! I trust that it doesn't sound like I am boasting because I am not. I know that the hand of the Lord has been upon our marriage from day one, and therefore, my boast is in Him.

I'm also grateful for our mantra this year, *Understanding the Kingdom of Heaven in 2011,* as the premise of this book fits right into it. Bear in mind that whenever there is a kingdom, there must be a king. The king of a kingdom sets the rules and regulations that are to be adhered to under his domain. Now we understand that there are kings in this world and the people of that king are subject to his rulership. The Bible says in Acts 17:5-8, "But the Jews which believed not, moved with envy, took unto them certain lewd fellows of the baser sort, and gathered a company, and set all the city in an uproar, and assaulted the house of Jason, and sought to bring them out to the people. And when they found them not, they drew Jason and certain brethren unto the rulers of the city, crying, 'These that have turned the world upside down are come hither also; Whom Jason hath received: and these all do contrary to the decrees of Caesar, saying that there is another king, one Jesus." Jason received Jesus and declared that there was another king, the King of Kings whose name is Jesus. Since Jesus is the King of Kings, we are subject to His lordship and the rulership of His kingdom. In other words, what He says goes.

In Matthew 13:51-52 Jesus said to His disciples, "Have you understood all these things?" They said to Him, "Yes, Lord." Then He said to them, "Therefore every scribe instructed concerning the kingdom of heaven is like a householder who brings out of his treasure things new and old." The Wuest Translation says it this way, "Have you understood all these things? They say to Him, "Yes." And He said to them, "Because of this, every man learned in the sacred scriptures who has accepted the precepts and instructions with reference to the kingdom of heaven is like a man who is a master of a house, who is of such a character that he dispenses with hearty enjoyment out of his treasure-house, things new as to quality and also things mellowed with age by reason of use."

I have been tremendously blessed by this verse for our mantra, *Understanding the Kingdom of Heaven.* Jesus asked His disciples, did they understand what He was saying, so one of the first things that we learned and reviewed was what it means to have an understanding of something. To understand something is to submit to God's point of view on the matter. So, in essence, during this season of our lives, God is calling the Body of Christ to submit to His way of being and doing right. God is calling for us to grow to a place of maturity this year that we may out of our growth, grow His kingdom. It's all about Him!

Note how in Matthew 13:52 Jesus asked His disciples after giving them the seven kingdom parables in Matthew 13, "Have you understood all these things?" They responded, "Yes, Lord." As a born again believer, our response should always be, "Yes Lord," for it is indicative of His Lordship in our lives. If you are struggling in your marriage, or any other area for that matter, it means that He is not Lord in that area. If He is Lord and we understand, there should be a corresponding action. Our lives should be proof of His Lordship, as we purpose to glorify Him in every area. However, as I look into the eyes of many wives I don't see that Jesus is Lord in their relationship with their husband.

The eyes are the window to the soul and like it or not they tell what is *really* going on. I see so much frustration in the eyes of God's daughter's and I believe it is because many have failed to count the cost of what it really takes to be a kingdom minded wife. This is due to the fact that the main reason that many single women got married is because they primarily desired breath and britches. The problem with this is that now that these women are married, they have discovered that his breathe stinks in the morning too and sex does not pay the bills. Furthermore, they have no clue as to what it means to treat their husband like a king.

My endeavor, therefore in this book is to equip Christian wives through biblical principles on how to treat their husbands like a king. For some, this may be a challenge. For others, it will enhance their relationship with their husband because they already understand how to honor and respect their husband. No matter which category you find yourself in, it will require you to focus. Let me elaborate on this word "focus" through an acronym that the Lord gave me.

Fix your eyes on Jesus. First and foremost, in order to treat your husband like a king, you must fix your eyes on King Jesus. He is the Author and Finisher of your faith. You **cannot** look to the action or non-action of your husband to determine whether he deserves to be treated like a king. None of us deserve the goodness that the Lord bestows upon us all day and every day.

Therefore, it's not about what your husband is doing or not doing. It is all about the Lord Jesus Christ and you walking in obedience to Him.

Overcome the obstacles. As you fix your eyes on Jesus and walk in obedience to Him, He will give you the ability to overcome the obstacles in your marriage. I know that somewhere, somehow you received faulty information that promised you that once you got married that everything was going to be like a sweet walk in the park on a sunny Sunday afternoon. No! Marriage takes work and in order for you to overcome the obstacles, you have to remain focused. God has already given you all the keys you need to overcome. As a born-again believer, you have already overcome by the blood of the Lamb. Jesus has made you more than a conqueror!

Commune with the Lord. However, I do realize that sometimes, many times the warfare in marriage gets pretty intense. That is when you have to set your heart to commune with the Lord in prayer. The Bible declares that we are to always pray, pray without ceasing, continue in prayer, and to worry about nothing, but pray about everything (Luke 18:1, 1 Thessalonians 5:17, Colossians 4:2; Philippians 4:6). When we give our hearts to commune with Him in prayer, look at what the Word of God promises us in 1 John 5:14-15; "And this is the confidence that we have in Him, that, if we ask any thing according to His will, He heareth us: And if we know that He hear us, whatsoever we ask, we know that we have the petitions that we desired of Him." What an awesome privilege to commune with God in prayer.

Understand His Purpose. Through our communion with Him, He gives us the ability to understand His purpose for our lives during the different seasons of marriage. Yes, the Lord will give you an understanding of the seasons of your marriage. This is vitally important because if you don't understand the purpose of a thing, abuse is inevitable. God wants you to understand this season in your life as a wife so that you can fulfill His kingdom purpose in your marriage.

Stand on the Word. Finally, in order to remain focused on God's kingdom purpose, you have to stand on the Word. Stand means to remain steadfast, firm and fixed. Therefore as a woman of God, desiring God's best for your marriage, you must remain steadfast, firm and fixed upon the Word of God. I love how this is displayed in Joshua 1:8. It reads, "This book of the law shall not depart out of thy mouth; but thou shalt meditate therein day and night, that thou mayest observe to do according to all that is written therein: for then thou shalt make thy way prosperous, and then thou shalt have good success." You can make your own marriage prosperous by standing on the Word, being careful to obey all of it.

The Lord instructed me to add this exhortation on F.O.C.U.S. in the introduction of this book. I believe He did this because there are many of you who struggle in your relationship with your husband, let alone treating him like a king with honor and respect because you are not focused. In order to receive what the Spirit of the Lord is saying to you as you read, you must remain focused. I believe as you do, you will fully benefit from what I will be sharing with you and it will transform your marriage.

Well glory, it's time to begin our journey. Before we begin, I must say that this book was inspired by my king and boo Robert. He wrote a book in which I was the inspiration entitled, *Treat Her Like a Lady*[1]. It is an awesome book that will encourage and inspire husbands to love, locate, learn, lead, let their wives be who they are and lavish her. I have a wonderful husband and he really does purpose to do all those things for me. I'm not just saying this to make him sound like someone he is not. Besides if I did that, he would be a hypocrite and I would be a liar; neither of which we are. I speak the truth from a sincere heart and a pure conscience. I have a good man and God uses him to show me His love on a daily basis.

With that said, I want to let you know that I am a honored and privileged that you are taking time out to read what the Spirit of the Lord is saying through me. I trust you will be inspired and encouraged as I lay out some practical insights before you. I know you will be blessed and by the end of our journey, your marriage will be strengthened and you will be well equipped to treat your husband like a king!

Chapter 1

Revelation of the King

As we begin our journey, I first let's talk about the meaning of the word "revelation." I believe we need to start here, so as to establish a firm foundation for the rest of the material that will be presented to you in this book. Paul prayed this prayer in Ephesians 1:17, "That the God of our Lord Jesus Christ, the Father of glory, may give unto you the spirit of wisdom and revelation in the knowledge of Him." He went on in verse 18 in prayer asking that the eyes of their understanding would be enlightened so that they would know the hope of His calling.

This is one of the greatest prayers in the Bible because it is requesting for God to reveal who He is in order for us as His children to have an understanding of Him. If we don't understand Him then we can't properly relate to Him. If we can't properly relate to Him, then we can't properly relate to others. This is one of the main reasons why there is such a breakdown in relationships among Christians. A large number of God's children just don't understand or know the Lord as a loving, caring, sharing heavenly Father.

Rick Renner, in his book, *Sparkling Gems From the Greek*[2] explains "revelation" this way: "The word "revelation" is from the word *apokalupsis*. It refers to something that has been veiled or hidden for a long time and then suddenly, almost instantaneously, becomes clear and visible to the mind or eye. It is like pulling the curtains out of the way so you can see what has always been just outside your window. The scene was always there for you to enjoy, but the curtains blocked your ability to see the real picture. But when the curtains are drawn apart, you can suddenly see what has been hidden from your view. The moment you see beyond the curtain for the first time and observe what has been there all along but not evident to you — that is what the Bible calls a "revelation." Now apply the meaning of this word to the realm of spiritual truths. The truths we now grasp and enjoy were always there in the realm of the Spirit, but they were veiled — hidden to us. It wasn't the time for these truths to be revealed yet, so they remained obscured from our sight, even though they were always there. But once the right time came and the Holy Spirit removed the veil that obstructed our view, our minds instantly saw and understood. When this occurred, you and I had a revelation!"

When you think of this definition in the context of Ephesians 1:17-18, it helps us to realize that God wants us to have the ability to know and understand who He is so that we can have a better relationship with Him. His desire is for the veil to be pulled back from our mind in order to see Him for who He really is. Once this unveiling takes place, it will be manifested in the everyday lives of believers. This is an *apokalupsis*! You know you are flowing in it because the insecurities, inadequacies and old habits that plagued you are gone and you are living in His light, life and love.

It is evident in the Body of Christ that many are lacking revelation. It is displayed in the attitudes and actions of men and women, boys and girls, married and single people. If a single woman experiences God as a Father while single, then, chances are, when she gets married, she will be very fulfilled in her relationship with her husband. If a single man knows or shall I say, has a revelation of the love of the Father, he will have no problem loving his wife as Christ loves the church. However, it is evident that this revelation is missing because marriages are falling apart at the seams. Wives are looking to their husbands for safety, satisfaction and security which can only be found in the Lord. Husbands wrestle with the simple task of just loving their wives. Then there are the poor children who are subject to the lack of revelation in their parent's lives and they in turn end up repeating the cycle.

So, ladies, let's begin by asking ourselves, "Do I have a revelation of who the King of Glory is?" In order to treat our husband like a king, we need the covers pulled back in our minds in order to see who the King of Kings is. The Bible answers this question for us in Psalm 24:8 which reads, "Who is this King of glory? The LORD strong and mighty, the LORD mighty in battle." The King of glory is the Lord! Not only is He the Lord, He is the Lord God, strong and mighty in battle! He is the Lord, high and lifted up and more than able to do anything that is needed to be done in our lives. Nothing is too hard for our God! He is omnipotent, omniscient and omnipresent. He is an ever present help in trouble! He is our deliverer and developer. He is the one who gives us dominion! He is the Lord! He is our loving, caring sharing heavenly Father who delights in giving us the kingdom. He is God all by Himself and there is none other like Him. Hallelujah!

Since He is all of that and so much more, have you put your whole trust in Him? Is He your King, or are you subject to another authority? Have you put more trust in your husband than you have put in the Lord? Keep in mind that a king is one who has sovereign rule and control over everyone in his kingdom. Does the Lord have total rule and reign in your life? If He does, it should be reflected in your day to day actions and attitudes.

You see, when I got saved, I received Jesus as my Savior and Lord. Not only did I trust Him to save me, I trusted Him to give me a new way of doing things so that I could bring glory to Him. This was my frame of mind when I got married and it still is after 19 years of being married to my "big hunka burnin' love" Robert James Poole, Jr. I treat him like a king, because I have a revelation of the Lord as my King. I am living in His kingdom, and I desire to please Him in everything I do. Robert and I have shared our testimony that the success of our marriage is solely due to the fact that King Jesus is on the throne of our hearts and we live our lives to bring honor to Him.

So, what are you saying Sheila? What does all this mean? What I'm saying is that if you have a revelation of the King of Kings, He will give you the instructions in the Bible (the number one all time best seller marriage manual) on how to treat your husband like a king. The Bible has been the source of my instruction in treating Robert like a king. One of my favorite verses is found in Ephesians 5:33. I love how it reads in the Amplified version of the Bible: "However, let each man of you [without exception] love his wife as [being in a sense] his very own self; and let the wife see that she respects and reverences her husband [that she notices him, regards him, venerates, and esteems him; and that she defers to him, praises him and loves and admires him exceedingly]." In other words, we as wives should make it our business to treat our husbands like a king!

Okay, that's Bible, but what about my dead beat husband? Why should I treat him like a king when I can't even get him to take out the trash, let alone love me like Christ loves the church? Well, I'm glad you asked. I'm not sure if you are really going to like my answer, but if you let me, I can help you. I believe many women share these sentiments and feel they are justified in not honoring their husband because they are not honorable men.

In response to your question, I submit to you a question. What does the Word say? The Bible says in Ephesians 5:33 that the wife is to see that (in other words, make it your business or the other woman will) she reverences her husband. You just read this in the Amplified version, and please note this is a command given for the wife to carry out in obedience to the Lord. I also want to bring to your attention that this verse of scripture says nothing about the bad action or non action of your husband. His Lordship in your life says you must obey this scripture. I know it may seem like a hard task to carry out, but remember, you can do all things through Christ who strengthens you. I trust you picked up this book because you want

13

some solutions to the challenges you may be currently facing. Therefore, ask the Lord for His grace to carry out His Word in your life. Remember, God is giving you a revelation of His Kingship in your life so you can in turn treat your husband like a king.

Questions

1. According to the text, what is one of the greatest prayers in the Bible?
2. What does the word, "revelation" mean?
3. Who is the King of Glory?
4. Do you have a revelation of the King of Glory?
5. According to the text, wives should make it their business to do what?
6. Who will give you instructions on how to treat your husband like a king?
7. How does Ephesians 5:33 in the Amplified instruct you to treat your husband?
8. How does this verse apply to an unsaved or unruly husband?
9. Why did God give us wives a revelation of His Kingship?
10. Are you ready to learn how to treat your husband like a king?

Memory Verse: Psalm 24:8-10 (KJV) Who is this King of glory? The LORD strong and mighty, the LORD mighty in battle. Lift up your heads, O ye gates; even lift them up, ye everlasting doors; and the King of glory shall come in. Who is this King of glory? The LORD of hosts, he is the King of glory. Selah

Chapter 2

Hush! No Talking Zone

O kay my sisters, my friends (You are still my friends aren't you?) now we are going to build on our foundation of revelation. I say that because you can only go forward successfully from here in your relationship with your husband if you have a revelation and are walking in the Lordship of Jesus Christ. I know what I am about to share with you might cause your soul to rise up a bit, but, if Jesus is Lord you will tell your soul to shut up! Let sister soul girl know she is no longer in charge! King Jesus calls the shots now and He is teaching me how to treat my husband like a king! If you take charge, your soul girl will simmer down and follow the Word, will and wisdom of His way.

So, let me start off by asking you, what do a school zone, construction zone and a learning zone all have in common? First I will define them. A school zone is the area where the speed limit is reduced to fifteen to twenty-five miles an hour for the safety of the children coming and going to school. A construction zone is where work is being done on a building or roadway in which the speed is also reduced for the safety of the workers, drivers or pedestrians in the area. A learning zone is found in schools, homes or libraries where it is necessary that an atmosphere of learning is maintained at all times.

The thing that all three have in common is that when people are in these zones they have to take precautions and be aware of what is going on around in them at all times. Also it is necessary to obey the rules of these zones because it may cause harm to the ones working in or passing through these zones. If a person violates a school zone or construction zone by speeding, they are subject to higher fines than they would be if they were not in these zones.

With all that said, I want to introduce to you the *No Talking Zone*. This is not just a space or room in your home. It is not a place you can go to and know that you are not supposed to talk. The *No Talking Zone* is a dimension that you must learn to walk in, because the signs may pop up in your spirit at any given time. You have to be sensitive to the leading of the Holy Spirit in this zone because violators are subject to minor and/or major consequences. Your soul may not like this zone, especially if she never knew it existed. However, it is imperative that you learn to live in it in order to promote peace wherever you are. Keep in mind the name of this zone in order to receive the revelation. God is trying to teach and train your soul to hush so that the wrong things don't come out of your mouth. The *No Talking Zone* is all about learning to keep your mouth shut.

I've been around some great women of God in my life. These women have mastered the art of living in the *No Talking Zone*. One thing in particular that I observe about them is how they relate to their husbands in the public arena whether large or small. I watch how they all are quiet in his presence yet reverently in tune to everything that he is saying. Now please don't misunderstand me to say that these women are robots under control, fearful to say anything. No, she is a picture of a woman of God making it her business to respect and reverence her husband by not running off at the mouth.

I have also been around some women of God who, quite frankly, just talk too much in public and in private. My husband and I have done quite a bit of marriage counseling and we have learned a lot from others powerful teaching on marriage. The one thing that we have discovered from both of these settings is that husbands really dislike it when their wives talk too much. Now, one would think that once you got the memo that your spouse, (the one you call king and boo) doesn't like you running off at the mouth you would be quiet. Once you got the memo that your husband doesn't like it when you tell your girlfriends *everything* that is going on in your home you would be quiet. One would think this would provoke you as a God fearing woman to bridle your tongue. Well, unfortunately, in the Body of Christ, wives are STILL talking when they should remain silent. Prayerfully you are not one of those women, but just in case, keep reading. I'm going to give you the Word of the Lord so that you can train yourself to hush in the *No Talking Zone*.

The Bible says in Proverbs 10:19, "In the multitude of words sin is not lacking: but he who restraineth his lips is wise." Proverbs 17:27-28 says, "He that hath knowledge spareth his words: and a man of understanding is of an excellent spirit. Even a fool, when he holdeth his peace, is counted wise: and he that shutteth his lips is esteemed a man of understanding." Ecclesiastes 5:3 declares, "For a dream cometh through the multitude of business; and a fool's voice is known by multitude of words." Need another verse? James 3:2 states, "For in many things we offend all. If any man offend not in word, the same is a perfect man, and able also to bridle the whole body."

After reading those few verses you may still find yourself talking and even saying, "You don't know who I live with. You don't know my husband." "I try to keep quiet, but some of the things he says just make me so mad, I just have to say something!" Okay, first of all, I don't need to know your husband and I did not ask you what you were *trying* to do. The Bible is clear on your instructions, no matter who your husband is. "Likewise, ye wives, be in subjection to your own husbands; that, if any obey not the word, they may without the word be won by the conversation of their wives; while they behold your chaste behavior coupled with fear" (1 Peter 3:1-2). The Living Bible reads verse 1 this way, "Wives, fit in with your husbands' plans; for then, if they refuse to listen when you talk to them about the Lord, they will be won by your respectful, pure behavior. Your godly lives will speak to them better than any words."

I'm sure you have read these verses before. Perhaps you have not. Either way, you are reading them now and accountable for what you have learned. I do understand that things on the home front can be quite challenging, BUT, the Word is more than able to equip you to overcome any challenge you face with your husband. Your role is not to *fix* your husband with your words (Remember the "O" of F.O.C.U.S.?). Let me say that again. Your job is not to *fix* your husband with your words. Your job is to obey God's Word in every area of your life and that includes your mouth. Ask the Lord to help you. Cry out to God and tell Him, I don't know how to not talk too much. Help me to bridle my tongue. I don't want to sin against You with my words. I guarantee that if you ask the Lord for help with a humble heart ready to change, He will come rushing to your aid. Then, the next time you are about to run off at the mouth, you will sense the Lord holding your tongue and remain silent. When this happens you can rejoice for the victory and be prepared for another opportunity until you have learned the art of tuning into K.Y.M.S. This stands for Keep Your Mouth Shut. It is the station when tuned into on a regular basis will create perpetual peace in your home.

My mother in the faith, Pastor Val said something at a women's retreat that I attended in December of 2002. She said, "It is a crime to forfeit your peace." That statement resonated in my heart and soul. I tell my spiritual daughters that I refuse to let anything disturb my peace. The two statements are parallel and confirm the thought that God wants His peace to guard our heart and soul in every area of our lives.

I said all that to say, if you are talking too much, namely about or to your husband in a negative way, you are disturbing his peace! You are creating an atmosphere of war, not peace in your home. You are spiritually charged with the crime of forfeiting peace with your husband, and are now sentenced to be a prisoner in your own home. Pastor Rob and I have counseled many couples who are locked up in their homes, simply because the wife (hopefully not you) will not hush!

How important is your peace to you? Furthermore, how important is your husband's peace to you? The Bible says in Romans 12:18, in the God's Word translation, "Do everything possible on your part to live in peace with everybody." In case you were wondering, your husband is a part of that everybody, so if saying something at that moment is going to upset the equilibrium of peace... be quiet! What you have to say is not that important if it is going to cause an argument.

Speaking of arguments, did you know that an argument is nothing more than a verbal fight? It is an exchange of words that is meant to harass, hurt or hinder the person the words are directed at. So, for the sake of peace, ask yourself, "Self, is what you are about to say going to cause me to forfeit my peace and disturb my husband's peace? Will your words be hurtful to your husband and provoke an argument? Will what you are about to say harass him and hinder his relationship with you, or worse yet with God? If you answered yes to any of these statements, tell yourself to shut up! Then say, I will not allow my mouth to cause my flesh to sin, and I will teach and train my mouth to hush in the *No Talking Zone.*

Another way of putting it is that you must learn the art of telling your soul, "Hush! This is a *No Talking Zone*. Violators are accountable to God." You must become skilled at living in the *No Talking Zone*. This will take some practice, but I believe that if you take the time to meditate and memorize the verses given in this chapter as well as any others that apply, you will find yourself being brought under subjection to them. Don't try to change. Trying involves no commitment! You know the last time you tried to lose weight, you gained and lost and gained and lost. Train for change. Set goals and put them into practice every day until you can successfully say that you are a living testament to the peace that comes from living in the *No Talking Zone*.

Before you read on to the next chapter, I want to give you one final nugget that I believe will help you. I'm going to share a bit of my personal testimony that will give some insight on perhaps why you may feel the need to speak up instead of hush up!

On March 10, 2009, I had a hysterectomy due to fibroids on my uterus. Prior to the surgery, I began having hot flashes which I thought was a result of peri-menopause. Well, come to find out, I was not in early menopause. It was actually fibroids that were causing my body to show forth those symptoms. As a result, I ended up having the surgery which I have recovered successfully from.

However, now two years after the surgery, I am going through the whole menopause thing! What in the world is that all about? Well, since I am fascinated by the medical field, especially obstetrics,

I took it upon myself to ask the questions and do the research to find out just what was going on with my body. I discovered that even though I did not have a complete hysterectomy, my estrogen levels were still low which cause me to have hot flashes, night sweats and mood swings.

I have found some herbs and spices (vitamins) to help with the hot flashes and night sweats. But, the mood swing thing was a whole different story! Not to mention that the hot flashes come quite unannounced making me a bit fussy (well, actually, very fussy) and I'm not the easiest person to be around at that moment. If anyone is not going to contribute to my not being hot then they are considered an enemy! I get snappy, irritable and touchy which disturbs the peace of all parties involved, including my husband.

Well, I had to pray about all of this, because I could not live my life causing everyone who is with me grief because I am hot! God was faithful and He has shown me some practical things to do so that I can go through this new phase of my life gracefully. Now, pretty much I try to make light of it all and if I'm too moody, I get somewhere by myself and relax.

So what does all of this have to do with the *No Talking Zone*? It has everything to do with it because, I believe that many times as a wife, the reason that she is going off at the mouth is because of a hormonal imbalance. Women cause problems in the church, in their homes and any other place they frequent simply because they are cyclical due to menstruation or menopause. No matter what the case is, you have to train your soul not to give in to your hormones.

Just because our estrogen levels are not normal does not give us as women of God the license to act up!

If you discover that this is the reason why you are violating the *No Talking Zone*, pray and ask God for His wisdom, will and way for you to overcome. The Bible declares that we are overcomers and more than conquerors (Revelations 12:11; Romans 8:37). It also says that the Greater One lives on the inside of us and that the same Spirit that raised Jesus from the dead is at work in our mortal bodies giving us life (1 John 4:4; Romans 8:11). There are other verses in the Bible that lets us know that as women we are no longer in bondage to Satan, sickness or sin. Therefore, I charge you, mighty woman of God, full of faith, power and victory that the promises of God belong to you and you can have victory in this area of your life! Find out where the specific verses are and write out a prayer and confession for you to begin speaking over your life. I promise you will walk out triumphant as you train your soul to live by every word that proceeds out of the mouth of God.

Let me again remind you of Proverbs 10:19, "In the multitude of words sin is not lacking, but he who restrains his lips is wise." Pause, ponder and pay attention to this verse and the following verses that I have listed for you. When you find yourself about to violate the *No Talking Zone*, rehearse, review and recite these verses instead. It is amazing how if the soul is at peace you won't sin with your mouth. So, take the time to read each of them carefully.

There are approximately 400 verses on peace. I will only list some of them for you.

- **Proverbs 3:1-2** - My son, forget not my law; but let thine heart keep my commandments: For length of days, and long life, and peace, shall they add to thee.
- **Proverbs 3:13-17** - Happy is the man that findeth wisdom, and the man that getteth understanding. For the merchandise of it is better than the merchandise of silver, and the gain thereof than fine gold. She is more precious than rubies: and all the things thou canst desire are not to be compared unto her. Length of days is in her right hand; and in her left hand riches and honour. Her ways are ways of pleasantness, and all her paths are peace.
- **Isaiah 9:6-7** - For unto us a child is born, unto us a son is given: and the government shall be upon his shoulder: and his name shall be called Wonderful, Counsellor, The mighty God, The everlasting Father, The Prince of Peace. Of the increase of his government and peace there shall be no end, upon the throne of David, and upon his kingdom, to order it, and to establish it with judgment and with justice from henceforth even forever. The zeal of the LORD of hosts will perform this.
- **Isaiah 26:3-4** - Thou wilt keep him in perfect peace, whose mind is stayed on thee: because he trusteth in thee. Trust ye in the LORD for ever: for in the LORD JEHOVAH is everlasting strength:
- **Isaiah 26:12** - LORD, thou wilt ordain peace for us: for thou also hast wrought all our works in us.
- **Isaiah 32:17-18** - And the work of righteousness shall be peace; and the effect of righteousness quietness and assur-

ance forever. And my people shall dwell in a peaceable habitation, and in sure dwellings, and in quiet resting places;

- **Isaiah 53:5** - But he was wounded for our transgressions, he was bruised for our iniquities: the chastisement of our peace was upon him; and with his stripes we are healed.
- **Jeremiah 33:6** - Behold, I will bring it health and cure, and I will cure them, and will reveal unto them the abundance of peace and truth.
- **Ezekiel 37:26-27** - Moreover I will make a covenant of peace with them; it shall be an everlasting covenant with them: and I will place them, and multiply them, and will set my sanctuary in the midst of them for evermore. My tabernacle also shall be with them: yea, I will be their God, and they shall be my people.
- **Nahum 1:16** - Behold upon the mountains the feet of Him that bringeth good tidings, that publisheth peace!
- **Mark 4:39-41** - And He arose, and rebuked the wind, and said unto the sea, Peace, be still. And the wind ceased, and there was a great calm. And He said unto them, Why are ye so fearful? How is it that ye have no faith?
- **Luke 1:78-79** - Through the tender mercy of our God; whereby the dayspring from on high hath visited us, To give light to them that sit in darkness and in the shadow of death, to guide our feet into the way of peace.
- **John 14:27** - Peace I leave with you, My peace I give unto you: not as the world giveth, give I unto you. Let not your heart be troubled, neither let it be afraid.

- **John 16:33** - These things I have spoken unto you, that in Me ye might have peace. In the world ye shall have tribulation: but be of good cheer; I have overcome the world.

- **John 20:19-21** - Then the same day at evening, being the first day of the week, when the doors were shut where the disciples were assembled for fear of the Jews, came Jesus and stood in the midst, and saith unto them, Peace be unto you. 20 And when He had so said, He shewed unto them His hands and His side. Then were the disciples glad, when they saw the Lord. 21 Then said Jesus to them again, Peace be unto you: as my Father hath sent me, even so send I you.

- **Acts 10:36** - The word which God sent unto the children of Israel, preaching peace by Jesus Christ: (He is Lord of all:)

- **Romans 2:10-11** - But glory, honour, and peace, to every man that worketh good, to the Jew first, and also to the Gentile: For there is no respect of persons with God.

- **Romans 5:1** - Therefore being justified by faith, we have peace with God through our Lord Jesus Christ:

- **Romans 8:6** - For to be carnally minded is death; but to be spiritually minded is life and peace.

- **1 Corinthians 14:33** - For God is not the author of confusion, but of peace, as in all churches of the saints.

- **2 Corinthians 13:11** - Finally, brethren, farewell. Be perfect, be of good comfort, be of one mind, live in peace; and the God of love and peace shall be with you.

- **Galatians 5:22-25** - But the fruit of the Spirit is love, joy, peace, longsuffering, gentleness, goodness, faith, meekness, temperance: against such there is no law. And they that are

Christ's have crucified the flesh with the affections and lusts. If we live in the Spirit, let us also walk in the Spirit.

- **Ephesians 2:14-18** - For He is our peace, who hath made both one, and hath broken down the middle wall of partition between us; Having abolished in His flesh the enmity, even the law of commandments contained in ordinances; for to make in Himself of twain one new man, so making peace; And that He might reconcile both unto God in one body by the cross, having slain the enmity thereby: And came and preached peace to you which were afar off, and to them that were nigh. For through Him we both have access by one Spirit unto the Father.
- **Ephesians 4:3** - Endeavoring to keep the unity of the Spirit in the bond of peace.
- **Philippians 4:9-6** - Be careful for nothing; but in everything by prayer and supplication with thanksgiving let your requests be made known unto God. And the peace of God, which passeth all understanding, shall keep your hearts and minds through Christ Jesus. Finally, brethren, whatsoever things are true, whatsoever things are honest, whatsoever things are just, whatsoever things are pure, whatsoever things are lovely, whatsoever things are of good report; if there be any virtue, and if there be any praise, think on these things. Those things, which ye have both learned, and received, and heard, and seen in me, do: and the God of peace shall be with you.
- **Colossians 3:15-16** - And let the peace of God rule in your hearts, to the which also ye are called in one body; and be ye thankful. Let the word of Christ dwell in you richly in all

wisdom; teaching and admonishing one another in psalms and hymns and spiritual songs, singing with grace in your hearts to the Lord.

- **1 Thessalonian 5:23** - And the very God of peace sanctify you wholly; and I pray God your whole spirit and soul and body be preserved blameless unto the coming of our Lord Jesus Christ.
- **Hebrews 12:14** - Follow peace with all men, and holiness, without which no man shall see the Lord:
- **James 3:18** - And the fruit of righteousness is sown in peace of them that make peace.
- **1 Peter 3:11-12** - Let him eschew evil, and do good; let him seek peace, and ensue it. 12 For the eyes of the Lord are over the righteous, and his ears are open unto their prayers: but the face of the Lord is against them that do evil.

Prayerfully these verses will help you learn to live victoriously in the *No Talking Zone*. I am confident that as you purpose to live out the truths presented in these verses you will see your life transformed by the power of the gospel. You will successfully, by the power of the Holy Spirit train your soul to hush in the *No Talking Zone*.

Questions

1. How can you go forward successfully in your relationship with your husband?
2. In your own words, define the No Talking Zone.
3. What does Proverbs 10:19 say?
4. According to the Word, how should you treat your husband even if he doesn't obey the Word?
5. What will equip you to overcome the challenges with your husband that you are faced with?
6. What station should you tune into to create a perpetual atmosphere of peace?
7. There are over 400 verses on "peace" in the Bible. What does that say about what the Lord wants for you?
8. Do you talk too much (You might want to ask a trusted friend, confidant or your husband to help you answer this truthfully)?
9. Have you violated the No Talking Zone today?
10. If so, what should you do about it?

Memory Verse: 1 Peter 3:1-2 (TLB) Wives fit in with your husbands' plans; for then, if they refuse to listen when you talk to them about the Lord, they will be won by your respectful, pure behavior. Your godly lives will speak to them better than any words.

Chapter 3

Don't Be a Nag

When something is annoying to me, I say that it makes my armpits itch. The funny thing about this is that I have this minor affliction at times that my left arm pit itches. No matter how much I scratch, it itches all the more. It's like an itch that can't be scratched and when it flairs up, it bothers me to no end! Ugghhhh! Many times, if the flair up is bad, the only thing that makes it stop is to clean it and put some anti-itch cream on it. Finally, relief!

It's sad to say that many wives make their husbands armpits itch. This type of wife is labeled in the Bible as a contentious woman. A contentious woman is one who is argumentative, belligerent, fussy and disagreeable. She is one who cannot be pleased and is very vocal about everything that she is not pleased about. She is compared to a leaky faucet and a rainy day. The Word says that she just can't be turned off! Look at what these verses in Proverbs say about a contentious woman or wife.

- Proverbs 19:13 A foolish son is the ruin of his father, and the contentions of a wife are a continual dripping.
- Proverbs 21:9 Better to dwell in a corner of a housetop, than in a house shared with a contentious woman.
- Proverbs 21:19 Better to dwell in the wilderness, than with a contentious and angry woman.
- Proverbs 25:24 It is better to dwell in a corner of a housetop, than in a house shared with a contentious woman.
- Proverbs 27:15-16 A continual dripping on a very rainy day and a contentious woman are alike; whoever restrains her restrains the wind, and grasps oil with his right hand.

Notice that in all of these verses, a contentious wife or woman is not one who is desirable to be around. As a matter of fact two of the verses state that it is better to be outside on top of the roof than to be inside with an argumentative woman. Now that is some kind of comparison. How can it be better to be outside, on top of a roof where one would be subject to all the elements of the weather than to be inside with a contentious wife? You know that husband must be in a bad way if he would rather be outside than inside with his wife!

The sad thing about this state of affairs is that this is the testimony of Christian husbands. They would rather be in some other, any other, uncomfortable place than to be in the company of their wife. How could this be so for a believer? If the Bible says all these negative things about a contentious wife, you would think one would line up and just obey God. Unfortunately, this is not so and many, many Christian homes are on the brink of ruin simply because of a contentious wife.

A nagging wife is pretty much the same as a contentious wife. A nagging wife is one who continually complains by accusing, attacking and annoying her husband. This woman always finds fault in her husband and makes sure he knows about it. Years before the term reached popularity, this type of person was called a shrew. It depicted a woman in a sharp, shrill voice badgering her husband and or children to do whatever they felt wasn't being done. A nag is one who excessively criticizes her husband to the point he wants to go live on the roof!

All of this negativity comes from being naggish and contentious. It would be one thing if nagging worked, but it doesn't. Nagging never produces desirable results for several reasons. It fosters bitter resentment and creates the feeling that nothing is ever good enough or acceptable. Nagging makes husbands feel controlled, not to mention the fact that it's demeaning, disrespectful, and puts him on the defense. When this type of woman (not you though) is looked at through the lens of God's Word, it is clear that she has some serious sin issues in her heart that need to be dealt with.

I remember about five years ago or so Keeba, one of my spiritual daughters, pulled me to the side. She had a question for me and really needed an answer. She said, "Pastor Sheila, can I talk to you for a minute?" I said, "Sure. What's up?" She said, "Doesn't my opinion count for something?" I said (with my eyebrows raised),

"Not if it is going to cause an argument." This same truth applies to your opinion if you are being a contentious nag. If in your opinion, you are all right and he is all wrong, and you make it your business to tell him, you are being a contentious nag.

Another time, Keeba called me again just complaining about how terrible her husband Jeff was. This was not the first time we had a discussion about how bad she felt her husband was. This particular day I had had enough. Finally I asked her how long they had been married and how long had she been unhappy. At that time they had been married for five years and she said that she had been unhappy for five years. So, I told her quite emphatically, "Get a divorce then. If he is that bad and you are that unhappy, get a divorce!" I left her speechless that day and later she told me she wondered what kind of pastor I was to tell her to leave her husband when the Bible says God hates divorce.

Now, I had never been in this couple's home, but I venture to say that she was a contentious nag. Her poor husband was probably just miserable and ready to pitch a tent outside on the roof just to get away from her. On and on she went for years until...well let me stop there for now and save the end of the story for another chapter. For right now I want to emphasize the point that this saved woman had no revelation of the gift God had given her. All she knew was how to be a nagging, fussing, belligerent, wife.

You may share this testimony, but, if you let me I can help you. However, if you aren't ready for help, you may want to put this book down for a few moments, days, weeks or even months. Why?

Because what I am about to share with you is not for the faint at heart. It is for the God-like woman who is ready for a radical change in her marriage through the power of the Word of God. If that is you, read on my sister! Strap up, hold on and whatever you do, don't let go! Deliverance, development and dominion await!

Let me start by reiterating the title of this chapter, DON'T BE A NAG! Now that you are all clear on what a nag is, for clarity sake, let's review. Merriam-Webster's Dictionary defines "nag" as, to find fault incessantly; complain; to be a persistent source of annoyance or distraction; to irritate by constant scolding or urging; badger, worry. Interestingly enough, this particular dictionary did not use this word in reference to a wife. However, when I read the definition, I know plenty of wives whose name could replace the word nag.

Of course I am not talking about any of you reading this right now. I'm referring to your girlfriend, neighbor or co-worker who fits this description. You know the one who says things like, "Sam, when are you going to start taking the trash out when I ask you? I told you that you can't leave trash in the can when it gets full. You are supposed to take it out right away." "John, you never pay the bills on time. I told you the bills need to be paid on the first and the fifteenth, not the second and the sixteenth. You are going to ruin our credit and we will never be able to get a new house." "Jim, what you need to do is read your Bible like Pastor. I thought I already explained to you that as the priest of the home you have to put God first. We are never going to get ahead in life if you don't put God first." "Frank, how many times do I have to tell you that the light bulb needs changed? I guess you won't be happy until one of the kids runs into the wall at night because they can't see." Poor Sam, John, Jim, and Frank. They can't get a moment's peace because their wives just nag, nag, nag.

Now let me paint another scenario with Frank and the light bulb. Or, better yet, let me tell you a true story that God used as a tool for my husband and I to teach the Light Bulb Syndrome. As many of you may know, Robert and I lived in St. Louis in the early years of our marriage. At that time I was a stay at home mom. One day I was visiting a friend who was also a stay at home mom. She told me that her job was to take care of the children and the home. Her husband's job was to go to work, provide for the family and pay the bills. She told me that if he doesn't pay the power bill and the lights get turned off, she will just sit in the dark or light candles before she goes out to pay the bill.

What in the world is that all about? I remember her telling me that over fifteen years ago and it has stuck with me. Now I tell women all the time, don't be a nag. If you asked him to pay the power bill, and for whatever reason he doesn't and the power gets turned off, break out the candles or the flashlights. He will get the picture when he comes home to a dark house!

This may be hard to wrap your head around, but the concept of the light bulb syndrome is this: If you asked him to change the light bulb, pay the bills or take the trash out, don't be going and doing it yourself. Also, don't be asking or telling him to do these things over and over and over again. He heard you the first time!

And let me tell you, if you had to ask or tell him to do it more than once, you are being a nag!

I told you this part wasn't going to be easy to digest, BUT how valuable is your peace? Do you want revelation knowledge on how to treat your husband like a king or do you want some other chick to do it for you? Yeah, I know you don't like that kind of talk. Most wives don't want some other woman to steal their man but when you are being a nagging, contentious wife, you are just pushing him right into the other woman's arms!

So, the next time he does something that makes you sit, soak and sour, be sweet and make some lemonade instead. What I mean is rather than nag about the light bulb being out, turn it into a candle light night! Light candles all throughout the house, turn on the mood music and dance the night away. It's not going to be dark forever! As a matter of fact, by the time you wake up in the morning you will have all the light you need. Well, what about all the other things that need power like the stove, refrigerator and microwave? The same thing applies. Make the best out of the situation. The power is not going to be off forever. Trust God. He will make a way out of no way. Haven't you heard that before? Well, how do you think you will learn that He will make a way out of no way unless you are in a situation that looks like there is no way out!

I trust at this point, if you have not done so already you have evaluated yourself to see if you are a nagging, contentious wife. 2 Corinthians 13:5 says, "Examine yourselves as to whether you are in the faith. Test yourselves." So, put your name in the definition of a nag and see if you find yourself there. If so, today is your day of deliverance. Repent and ask the Lord to forgive you and ask your husband to forgive you. Then, purpose in your heart to be at peace with all men, including your husband.

Let me leave you with this. I trust that there are not too many birds swirling around your head with this new revelation that the Lord wants to impart into you. I do realize that some husbands are difficult to deal with or perhaps even unsaved.

First of all, I want you to take a look at John 21:20-23. It says, "Then Peter, turning around, saw the disciple whom Jesus loved following, who also had leaned on His breast at the supper, and said, "Lord, who is the one who betrays You?" Peter, seeing him, said to Jesus, "But Lord, what about this man?" Jesus said to him, "If I will that he remain till I come, what is that to you? You follow Me." Then this saying went out among the brethren that this disciple would not die. Yet Jesus did not say to him that he would not die, but, "If I will that he remain till I come, what is that to you?"

Peter was walking with the Lord and wanted to know about what the Lord was going to do with John. Jesus told him, "What is that to you?" In other words Jesus told Peter, "That is none of your business. You just be sure to do what I am telling you to do." Your husband may not be the stellar husband. Ok, so maybe your lights get turned off several times a year because of his negligence. Well, I say to you like Jesus said to Peter, "What does that have to do with you?" You just be sure that you are being obedient to what the Lord is telling you to do.

So, what is He telling you to do? What does the Word say your response should be in these types of situations? Proverbs 15:1- A soft answer turneth away wrath: but grievous words stir up anger. Proverbs 15:28 - The heart of the righteous studieth to answer: but the mouth of the wicked poureth out evil things. 1 Thessalonians 4:11 - And that ye study to be quiet, and to do your own business, and to work with your own hands, as we commanded you. James 1:19-20 - Wherefore, my beloved brethren, let every man be swift to hear, slow to speak, slow to wrath: For the wrath of man worketh not the righteousness of God. Romans 12:18 - If it be possible, as much as lieth in you, live peaceably with all men. 1 Peter 3:1-2 Likewise, ye wives, be in subjection to your own husbands; that, if any obey not the word, they also may without the word be won by the conversation of the wives; While they behold your chaste conversation coupled with fear.

As I said before, I do realize that some husbands are a bit difficult to deal with and sometimes there are things that need to be said. However, there is wisdom in the will, work, and way of the Lord which involves *how* and *when* things are said. The above scriptures teach that.

One day, Robert and I were going on vacation to Jamaica and we needed to get to the airport. He was with our son at a college orientation meeting and I was at home getting the rest of my things packed. The plan was for us to meet at the airport and get someone to take our car home. Regina, one of our spiritual daughters was going to take me to the airport and have her son meet her there to take her car home while she drove our car home.

While on the way to the airport, I called Robert and asked him where he wanted to meet us, so we could make the exchange/drop off. I suggested that we meet at the short term parking lot. He said no that he wanted me to call him when I got close to UNLV and we could swing by where he was. I was a bit uncomfortable about this, but I said ok. As we were driving down the freeway getting close to our exit, he called and asked where we were. I told him and asked, "Do you want to just meet us in the short term parking?" He said, "Okay, let's just meet there." Regina looked over at me and said, "I like how you handled that."

I had the opportunity to be fussy. We were both a bit edgy since it was coming up on the time we needed to be at the airport. I knew this was not the time to demand he do it my way. The best thing to do was to re-present the matter to him peaceably to see if he would agree; and he did. We met at the short term parking. Regina had someone to drive her car home, she drove our car home and we made our flight on time with the peace of God in our hearts.

After nineteen years, this is how Robert and I still function. I have purposed in my heart from the very beginning to obey God in everything, including my marriage. The results have been wonderful, and to God be the glory we have never had an argument. There have been plenty of opportunities to argue and there have been things that he has done that I have not liked. Nevertheless, I made a conscious choice to walk out the Word.

With that in mind, let me take you to the Scriptures to find out what you can do instead of being a nag. The opposite of nagging is encouragement. The epitome of encouragement is found in Ephesians 5:33. Let's look at it in the Amplified Bible. "However, let each man of you [without exception] love his wife as [being in a sense] his very own self; and let the wife see that she respects and reverences her husband [that she notices him, regards him, honors him, prefers him, venerates, and esteems him; and that she defers to him, praises him, and loves and admires him exceedingly]."

What does all this mean? It could be summed up in three words; respect your husband. I preached a message years ago entitled *Stand By Your Man*. In this message, one of the things that I talked about was that a man's deepest need is not love (like a woman), but respect. Ephesians 5:33 lays out how you as a godly woman can stand by your man and respect, not nag him.

These definitions were taken from many sources and include my additions. They are in the order that they are listed in the verse in the Amplified translation. Take time out to really pause, ponder and pay attention to what these words mean.

- Notice – pay attention to; observe, recognize
- Regard – gaze on steadily; attention or care; respect; consider

- Honor – high respect; exalted position, confer honor on, prize, value.
- Prefer – choose; like better; favor; be partial to. (Romans 12:10)
- Venerate – regard with deep respect, devotion and admiration (warm approval)
- Esteem – have a high regard for; formal consider; respect; favor; cherish; hold dear, value, treasure, appreciate.
- Defer – yield or make concessions; give in, submit; comply, acquiesce (agree quietly).
- Praise – express warm approval or admiration of; compliment
- Love – deep affection, fondness, sexual passion; sexual relations; delight in, admire greatly, cherish.
- Admire – Regard with approval, respect, or satisfaction; wonder at, delight in.

All these are to be done EXCEEDINGLY—very exceptionally, remarkably, excessively, greatly, enormously. WHY? Because a man's deepest need is respect. Respect means to admire, value, look up to, revere, heed, obey, attend to; defer to. Now, let me just drop this little tidbit of information on you before we get to it a few chapters later. Respect for some men is spelled SEX and lots of it!

I guarantee you that if you process this word through Joshua 1:8, it will deliver you from being a nag. Then you will be developed into the greatest source of encouragement for your husband so the two of you can walk in dominion in your marriage! Isn't that good news?

Remember, you don't win your husband over by being a nag. You win him over by your chaste behavior, not saying a word! So today allow this word to develop you. Purpose in your heart to cultivate an atmosphere of peace in your heart and in your home. Give your husband a break and walk upright before the Lord. Heed the call. Obey the charge. Don't be a nag! Treat him like a king so that you can rightly represent the King of Kings!

Questions

1. What are the five verses listed in Proverbs in reference to a contentious wife?
2. Nagging produces what negative results?
3. According to the text, what is the concept of the light bulb syndrome?
4. What three words sum up Ephesians 5:33?
5. What is the Biblical way to win your husband over?
6. Is nagging disrespectful? Why?
7. Does your husband think you are a nag? (You might want to ask him this one.)
8. If he does, what should you do about it?
9. Have you ever been in a situation where you were the one being nagged?
10. Did those nagging you have positive or negative effects on you?

Memory Verse: 1 Peter 3:1-2 (KJV) Likewise, ye wives, be in subjection to your own husbands; that, if any obey not the word, they also may without the word be won by the conversation of the wives; 2 While they behold your chaste conversation coupled with fear.

Chapter 4

Submit!

It Will NOT Kill You

Our son Joshua was the valedictorian at his high school graduation. Glory! Of course we sat there as proud parents as he gave his valedictory speech. He said all his thank you's and what nots, but his most profound statement was given to the children who would be returning to the school in the fall. He said, "There is nothing wrong with living right." I tell you, when he said that, Proverbs 23:24-25 was brought to life. "The father of the righteous will greatly rejoice, and he who begets a wise child will delight in him. Let your father and your mother be glad, and let her who bore you rejoice." We as his parents truly rejoiced as such wisdom came forth from our son.

I said all that to say that, ladies, there is nothing wrong with just submitting yourself to your husband as commanded by the Lord in His Word. You do the research and tell me, if you can, of one woman in the Bible who the Lord struck down for being submissive. Tell me if you can of any god-fearing woman that you know or have known that you attended their funeral because they submitted. Well, let me save you the trouble. Such a woman does not exist!

Ephesians 5:22, "Wives submit to your own husbands as to the Lord." and Ephesians 5:33, "Nevertheless let each one of you in particular so love his own wife as himself, and let the wife [see] that she respects [her] husband." are not suggestions that a Christian woman should obey when it's convenient. They are commands from the Lord to be carried out by every Christian wife. Failure to walk out these verses is sin.

Why does the Bible not command the wife to love the husband? That's simple. Love is not an issue for women because it is in the make-up of a woman to love. Women don't have a problem loving—they desire to be loved. However, love is not a man's deepest need.

What is the man's deepest need? As I said in the previous chapter, it is respect. This is why the woman is commanded on four different occasions in the New Testament to submit to the husband. Submission shows respect.

- **1 Corinthians 14:34** - Let your women keep silence in the churches: for it is not permitted unto them to speak; but they are commanded to be under obedience, as also saith the law.

50

- **Ephesians 5:22-23** - Wives, submit yourselves unto your own husbands, as unto the Lord. For the husband is the head of the wife, even as Christ is the head of the church: and He is the Saviour of the body. Therefore as the church is subject unto Christ, so let the wives be to their own husbands in everything.
- **Colossians 3:18** - Wives, submit yourselves unto your own husbands, as it is fit in the Lord.
- **1 Peter 3:1** - Likewise, ye wives, be in subjection to your own husbands; that, if any obey not the word, they also may without the word be won by the conversation of the wives.

In each of the above verses "wives submit" (which carries the connotation of continued repeated action not based on the action or non-action of the husband) is commanded because of a woman's natural inclination to control the husband. Genesis 3:16 says, "Unto the woman he said, I will greatly multiply thy sorrow and thy conception; in sorrow thou shalt bring forth children; and thy desire shall be to thy husband, and he shall rule over thee."

I want to park for a few moments and expound on the latter part of Genesis 3:16. I believe that this portion of scripture can be summed up in the thought that was birthed during the feminist movement in the late 60's and 70's. There was even a song that many women sang loud and proud to let the men know there is nothing that you do that I cannot do. You have heard it said, "Anything you can do I can do better." This statement from a wife gives the connotation that she can lead just like, if not better than, her husband.

The English Standard Version Study Bible Commentary[3] brings clarity to this thought. It says, "Your desire shall be for your husband, and he shall rule over you." These words from the Lord indicate that there will be an ongoing struggle between the woman and the man for leadership in the marriage relationship. The leadership role of the husband and the complementary relationship between husband and wife that were ordained by God before the fall, have now been deeply damaged and distorted by sin. This especially takes the form of inordinate desire (on the part of the wife) and domineering rule (on the part of the husband). The Hebrew term here translated "desire" (*teshuqah*) is rarely found in the OT. But it appears again in Genesis 4:7, in a statement that closely parallels Genesis 3:16 —that is, where the Lord says to Cain, just before Cain's murder of his brother, that sin's "desire is for you" (i.e., to master Cain), and that Cain must "rule over it" (which he immediately fails to do, by murdering his brother, as seen in Genesis 4:8).

Similarly, the ongoing result of Adam and Eve's original sin of rebellion against God will have disastrous consequences for their relationship: (1) Eve will have the sinful "desire" to oppose Adam and to assert leadership over him, reversing God's plan for Adam's leadership in marriage. But (2) Adam will also abandon his God-given, pre-fall role of leading, guarding, and caring for his wife, replacing this with his own sinful, distorted desire to "rule" over Eve. Thus one of the most tragic results of Adam and Eve's rebellion against God is an ongoing, damaging conflict between husband and wife in marriage, driven by the sinful behavior of both in rebellion against their respective God-given roles and responsibilities in marriage."

This is seen when the wife makes comments like, "The only reason we are out of debt is because I took over the bills." "Our finances were a mess when my husband was taking care of them." "I told him time and time again that just because he is the man doesn't mean he has to handle the money." "It's obvious from our constant struggles with money that he doesn't have a clue about what he is doing." I know that you may not say these exact words, but many times, and most of the times these words are displayed loud and clear through your actions.

It's the sin nature of a woman to want to control her husband. That is why the Bible has much to say about a wife and submission. It is important to understand that God ordained the preeminence of man. However, this does not mean that the woman is inferior to man (Genesis 1:27, Galatians 3:28). There are just designated functions for a husband and designated functions for a wife, which man cannot change because GOD has ordained them. We are all equal before God yet our functions and responsibilities differ. Women subject themselves to God, job, boss, government etc., but many fail to subject themselves to their husbands due to the fallen nature. In order to reverse the curse we must walk according to 2 Corinthians 5:17 and Romans 6:4.

So, how does a woman submit to or respect her husband? First let's look at "submission" defined. According to the Strong's Dictionary it means to arrange under; subordinate; to yield to one's admonition or advice; to obey. The Oxford Dictionary says it means to cease resistance; give way; yield, surrender, give in, agree, respect, subject. The simplest way for a woman to submit to her husband is to yield to him in whatever capacity necessary. This may mean being quiet when you want to speak, allowing him to make the decisions for the household, whether you agree with them or not, or quite frankly, not bossing him around telling him what you think he should do. In this way you show that you respect him and trust his judgment. Also it shows the heart of a woman who trusts God, especially when she may have a husband that is not living his life according to the Word of God.

Now that you are aware of what the Word has to say on the matter (although I have a strong inclination that you have heard them before), it is your responsibility to obey. God did not place these verses in the Bible for your consideration. No. He placed them in there as a command to you that should prompt your immediate obedience out of love and respect *for the Lord.* You are accountable to God for what you know and to not do what you know to do; according to the Bible, it is a sin (James 4:17).

The Bible declares in Isaiah 1:18-20, "Come now, and let us reason together," says the LORD, "Though your sins are like scarlet, They shall be as white as snow; Though they are red like crimson, They shall be as wool. If you are willing and obedient, you shall eat the good of the land; But if you refuse and rebel, you shall be devoured by the sword"; For the mouth of the LORD has spoken." God was not asking us to present our case before Him in this verse. What He is actually instructing us to do is to come to our senses based upon our sinful nature and see that He is right and we are wrong. Once we fully comprehend this, we are brought to a place to decide whether we will obey the Word of God or not. The blessings come to the willing AND obedient. You do understand that you can be willing and not obedient or obedient and not willing. We show our love for the Father by simply obeying Him because obedience is the highest form of love. Now, if you choose not to obey, well, the Bible is clear. You will be devoured. Perhaps you may find yourself having all kinds of challenges in your life, including, but not limited to, your marriage. Have you ever considered that the reason why all hell is breaking loose in your life is because you refuse to submit to your husband? If so, today is the day for you to repent and make mid-term corrections. I mean, you tell me, would you rather eat the good of the land or be devoured by the sword? Seems pretty straight forward to me, yet as a pastor, I encounter countless women who daily struggle with submission and have struggled for many years in spite of what the Word of the Lord says.

With that I say, SUBMIT! It will not kill you! The same women who struggle with submission don't know any who have died because they have submitted to their husband. I know it may be a struggle, but your struggle is not with your husband, it is with the Lord. Now let me tell you this, you will continue to have stress, struggle and strain in your marriage if you do not submit your husband. Besides, you *begged* God to give you a husband, so submit to the husband that you have whether He gave him to you or not. Remember, your submission has nothing to do with the action, or non-action of your husband. It is a command of the Lord and it will be in your best interest to obey.

Let me leave you with this final thought on submission to ease and comfort your heart. God in the beginning created both man and woman in His likeness and image and He gave both of them dominion. However, their dominion was not over one another. God never intended for your husband to rule over you like a tyrant, neither did He intend for you to rule over your husband. He ordained the husband to be the head and for the wife to submit. Keep in mind that this does not mean that you are to be subservient to your husband or that you are less important than he is. It means that you, out of obedience to God, are to willfully come under your husband's headship.

Questions

1. Will it kill you to submit?
2. What is the command given in Ephesians 5:22?
3. When a wife submits to her husband what does it show?
4. What is man's deepest need?
5. What is the Strong's definition of submit?
6. What is the Oxford Dictionary's definition of submit.
7. Based upon those two definitions, are you submitted to the Lord?
8. Do you have a problem submitting to your husband? Why or why not?
9. Does submission mean subservience? Explain.
10. Is this helping you?

Memory Verse: Colossians 3:18 (AMP) Wives, be subject to your husband's [subordinate and adapt yourselves to them], as is right and fitting and your proper duty in the Lord.

Chapter 5

Whatever You Like

Remember the 1988 comedy film, *Coming to America*[4]. The movie was written from a story by Eddie Murphy and the screenplay was written by David Sheffield and Barry W. Blaustein (a little movie trivia for you). Young Prince Akeem was heir to the throne of Zamunda, a fictitious country in Africa. He was coming into his own identity and he was tired of being pampered. The last straw was when his parents presented him with his bride-to-be, Imani Izzi (Did you know that was her name? I didn't!), who was played by Vanessa Bell.

Anyway, the scene that stands out for me in the whole movie is when he asks to talk to his bride-to-be in private. They leave the presence of the King, Queen and their guests and go into a room to the side of the royal throne. He opens the door for her and he closes it behind her after the train of her dress is completely in the room. He then proceeds to try and find out what she likes.

He begins by stating that since they were going to be married they should get to know each other first. Her response was that she had been trained to serve him since birth. He knows and understands that but persists in asking about her because he wants to know what she likes. So he asks Imani, "What do you like?" She responded bowing with her arms out, "Whatever you like." Not satisfied with her answer, he then asks her, "What kind of music do you like?" She said again, bowing with her arms out the same as before, "Whatever kind of music you like." He knows that she has been trained to like what he likes, but further asks, "What is your favorite food?" She responded in the same manner, "Whatever food you like." Well, you know how the rest of that scene goes. It ends with her leaving the room hopping on one foot and barking like a dog. God doesn't want you to hop around on one foot and bark like a dog for your husband. However, I do believe it would please the heart of the Father if every now and then you would just bow before you husband with your arms out saying, "Whatever you like."

For some, this may be no problem as you are seeking ways to please your husband. For some this whole concept may be a thorn in your side because you didn't get married to meet his needs. You got married to have your needs for affection, attention and affirmation to be met. If this is your testimony, you found out quick, fast and in a hurry that sometimes it takes faith to say, "Whatever you like," especially if your husband is not the easiest guy to get along with.

This is why marriage is not for the spiritually immature, nor the faint at heart. This is why marriage is not for someone who is so needy that the only person's needs that are important to be met are her own. This is why before you get married, it is paramount to be secure, satisfied and submitted to the Lord, so that your ultimate goal and purpose is to please God. If you don't have a problem pleasing God, you will have no problem pleasing your husband.

I know, I know, you are not married to Prince Akeem and your husband is not the sole heir of Zamunda. However, give the brother his props! Take time out to find out the things he likes and purpose in your heart to do them. For example, find out what his favorite meal is and cook it for him. If he likes homemade baked goodies from scratch, get to cracking the eggs, sifting the flour *and* creaming the butter and sugar to the tune of his favorite cake. Here's another one for you. Ask him what he likes to see you wearing in public and in private. Then, wear it and get rid of the things he tells you that he doesn't like. I'm telling you that if you would just take a little time to find out what he likes, you won't even have to tell him what you like. The gifts, goodies and gestures of love will be so abundant that you will find yourself tripping over one and falling into the next!

Contrary to popular belief, there are specific things that men like and need. Bride-to-be Imani was trained and spent her whole life studying a man she had never met just to please him. This woman is from a movie based on fictional characters, but I believe every husband would love it if his wife would just take a little time to find out what he likes and go out of her way to make sure that it happens for him.

So, now I'm going to talk about in some detail, things that husbands like. As I said before, they do have specific things that they like and it would be in your best interest to find out what they are. I came up with a list of ten things that husbands like. Initially I thought to share what men like. However, as a wife, your concern should not be about what men like, but what YOUR husband likes. Always remember that the other woman has no problem finding out what pleases your husband. Therefore, it behooves you to handle your business and get to finding out what he likes.

This list is not in any particular order of importance, because your husband may like something more than another husband. The key here is to allow this list to remind you that your husband has wants, needs, desires, likes and dislikes. Talk with your husband so you can find out exactly what is most important to him.

Number one: Husbands like for their wives to look nice. This should be pretty obvious since men are visual by nature. They are aroused, or turned on by what they see. I remember living in St. Louis and going through long periods of depression. During those times, I really didn't care what I looked like. I wouldn't take time to fix my hair up or wear cute clothes except on Sundays. Throughout the week, I would wear big t-shirts, big shorts and I would wear my hair in a pony-tail *a lot*. It was to the point where the few times that I did go to the beauty salon, my hair stylist would ask me did I wear make-up or have contacts. She would encourage me to take the time to make myself pretty. I heard her, but I wasn't quite feeling her.

I'm not quite sure when I got the revelation, but I know that by the time we got back to Vegas and began pastoring, I had to be sure I had my stuff together. Every Sally that comes to church is not saved and I am fully aware that the pastor is a target (The anointing is attractive)! Therefore, I make it my business to be a constant vision of loveliness for my hubby! I keep the hair, make-up, nails, clothes and weight together! I want him to get weak at the knees every time he looks at me! No sassy Sally with an unsanctified spirit has a chance with my king! Neither should she with yours. So go out of your way to look nice for your husband. He really likes it when you do!

Number two: They like a good meal. You have heard it said before, "The way to a man's heart is through his stomach." I don't know who said that first and I'm sure they said it a long time ago. Nevertheless, you and I both know that husbands love it when their wives can throw down in the kitchen!

I remember when I cooked for Robert for the first time. We were still single and I was about to move back to Phoenix. At that time, I knew he was my husband but he didn't know I was his wife. I asked him what he would like for me to fix. He asked me did I know how to cook chicken and dumplings and I said yes. I recall preparing that meal for him like it was yesterday.

At the time and unbeknownst to me, he told his mom, "If she can cook chicken and dumplings, I will marry her!" Well, that was one of the best pots of chicken and dumplings that I had ever prepared at the time and he loved it!

He didn't ask me to marry him after dinner that night, but we did get engaged a few days later. Ever since that time, I have purposed in my heart to cook to please my husband. I was born and raised in Pittsburgh, and Rob's family is from the south. My cooking style was quite different than what he was used to so, I made it my business to find out what he liked, how he liked it and fixed it just the way he liked it. I decided early on that I was not going to have my husband running back to his mama's house for a good meal.

After nineteen years of being married, my efforts have paid off. Now, he absolutely loves my cooking and prefers it above all others. Therefore, if you know you are not your husband's preferred chef, it would behoove you to get with his mother, take some classes, tune into the cooking channel or something! Your husband's belly is calling your name and waiting for you to fill it with some delicious meal! Give Jiffy and the processed foods a break. Find out what he likes and get to clanging the pots!

Number three: They like a clean home. This goes without saying, and I must admit that cleaning is not on the top of my most favorite things to do. That's why at this stage in my life, I am grateful to have the resources available to me to have someone come in and clean for me!

You may not have these resources, but you can do what you need to do to have the house tidy for your husband, especially when he comes home from work. You should do whatever you can to create an atmosphere of peace in your home, and part of that is having things picked up. You may have small children, but you can still do everything within your means to keep things in order in your home.

I have read books and heard stories of how a wife should keep her home clean. That is not what I am trying to do here. I just want to bring to your attention that your husband does like a clean home and you can do what needs to be done to see to it that it is clean. If you have several small children, or one small child this may be a bit of a challenge. Therefore, talk to your husband and let him know that you are working out a plan to create a haven in your home. In that, let him know that you will at least be sure that certain rooms are clean before others, like the bedroom or the living room. The bedroom because a cluttered space is not very romantic and the living room because it is probably the first room he comes into when he comes home.

Whatever room you choose, the point is this; your husband likes a clean home. Do what it takes to honor him by keeping your home nice and neat whether he asks you about it or not. If he does happen to have to ask you about it, don't get an attitude. Just say, "Whatever you like," and get to cleaning!

Number four: They like to watch sports. I know you know this! In fact, if you think about it, there are not too many husbands that you know who don't like sports. The flip side of this truth is that most women do not like sports. My hat goes off to the few ladies who love sports just as much as their husbands and can eat, sleep and drink sports with their husband. What an added bonus to that relationship!

For the rest of us who can take them or leave them, it wouldn't hurt to sit and watch a game or two throughout the season. Robert's favorite sport to watch is football. For me, I'd almost rather be driving in a snow storm that to sit at home and watch football. HOWEVER, I have had to tell my soul a thing or two over the years. Besides, if football is important to him, the least I can do is show some interest in what he is interested in.

Now, what I do from time to time is just sit in the room with him while a game is on and do something else like read, crochet or take a nap. There have been a few times after church that I have laid down to take a nap and he would be headed out the room. I would ask him to stay in the room with me until I fell asleep with the game on. I just wanted to be in his presence. Those have been really sweet times, even though it would seem like the *same* game had been on for five hours!

Number five: Not only do they like to watch sports, they like to play sports. Over the years, I think my big hunka burning love has only played football and softball with organized teams. There have been other times that he has gone out to play basketball with some of the guys. Here of late, he has taken up a bit of golfing and seems to enjoy that as well.

I do realize that some husbands are into playing sports more than others. If you feel like your husband plays too much, have him read *Treat Her Like a Lady*. It will help him balance some things out. However, don't confuse him wanting to play whatever sport every once in a while for not wanting to spend time with you. You need to be secure enough in yourself to give him this time to do what he likes to do. While he is doing his thing, go out and do something you enjoy. Or, better yet, fix him a special meal, clean the house and be waiting on the couch for him in some cute nightie! I tell you he will surely like that! Just be prepared to finish what you started!

Number six: Are you ready to finish what you started? You do realize that after he comes in from playing whatever, smells the food as soon as he opens the door, and sees you there in all your glory he is going to do it! Do what? He is going to want to do the horizontal polka, the smoothie, the milk shake or whatever you want to call it because **your husband *loves* sex!**

It is amazing to me that this is a known fact to every wife, but many wives fail to fulfill their husband's desire in this area. I have devoted a whole chapter to this subject, so I am not going to spend much time here. However, I will say that the other woman is always ready, willing and able to give it up for YOUR husband. So, don't allow your flesh to cause you to sin by not giving your husband what he likes in the bedroom and that is sex.

Number seven: Not only does your husband like sex, he likes to see you in sexy undergarments. Now before you get all twitterpated (that is a word me and my sister made up that means wound up or uptight), it is okay for you Christian woman, to wear cute underwear. The other woman is wearing it to draw your husband away from you so you better find something other than flannel to wear to keep him close to you!

This is also a topic I will cover in depth in another chapter. However, I will say a few things to create a sense of anticipation for the chapters to come. Husbands like to see their wives in matching bra and panty sets. With this in mind, you should (if you haven't already), purchase a set and let him see you getting dressed. When he mentions it, just smile and say, "You like? I bought it special for you." I'm telling you, it will warm the very cockles of his heart just knowing you had him in mind when you picked that little number up!

Number eight: Husbands like to be complimented on the way they look. This is important because along with the last two things that I mentioned that your husband likes, the other woman will also go out of her way to tell your man; yes *your man* that he looks and smells good all the time!

When we lived in St. Louis, Robert worked on the Casino Queen which was a riverboat on which people could come and gamble. I called the place Sodom and Gomorrah because all kinds of lasciviousness, wickedness and debauchery went on in that place. I can recall three separate occasions of women who blatantly flirted with him, *knowing* that he was married. The nerve of those women!

I was shell shocked at first that they would do such a thing, but such is the way of sinners. As I said before, somewhere along the line I got a revelation. I'm glad I got it sooner than later because now with him being a pastor, he is still a target for other women to try to roll up on him. Therefore, since I am a very wise woman, I make it my business to let him know how fine he is to me. I have a good looking husband and I make sure I tell him in private and public.

So, with that said, be sure to tell your husband you like how he looks. Let him know publicly and privately that he looks good to you. Don't spare any words and be creative. In that way, no matter where he is or what some other woman says to him it will not move him because you have already filled him up with how good he looks to you.

Number nine: Husbands like their space. When Joshua and Shekinah were babies, I was a stay at home mom. I remember one day while driving somewhere, I was listening to a preacher on the radio talking about marriage. In this particular segment, he discussed the importance of a man having his space.

One of the ways he shared that a wife can give her husband space is to let him unwind when he comes home from work before you bombard him with all the things that have gone on in your day whether good or bad. Little Johnny or Susie may have driven you up the wall that day and then swung all the way to the other side of the pendulum and did something so great you couldn't wait to tell your husband. Not to mention the fact that your mother upset you and the creditors are calling. You may feel like an overfilled water balloon about to pop when he walks through the door, but hold your peace! Go pray; prepare dinner or something for about thirty minutes or so to give him a chance to get the job off of him. Give him his space to unwind, read his Bible or just vegetate for a while.

Once he has settled in for the evening, then, begin to tell him about your day.

Remember, your husband likes his space. Come to think about it, don't you like your space too? No one wants to feel smothered in a relationship. So, purpose in your heart to give your husband ample opportunities to do things that he likes with or without you.

Number ten: Husbands like peace and quiet. This one falls under the *No Talking Zone*. We covered this topic in depth in chapter two and I trust that you picked up what I was putting down in that chapter. In fact, I also touched on it in chapter three, *Don't Be a Nag*. I am not trying to be redundant but, the Bible does say in 2 Peter 1:12, "Wherefore I will not be negligent to put you always in remembrance of these things, though ye know them, and be established in the present truth." God wants you to be established in this truth that your husband likes peace and quiet. Therefore, as much as has to do with you, be at peace with him.

With that all said, if you find yourself talking too much, too loud or at the wrong time, just hush. Your husband likes your quiet and peaceable side. In fact he cherishes it as one of your finest qualities! Now I know this may be a faith statement for some, but hey, you are a mighty woman of faith. Honor your husband today and as much as has to do with you, purpose to walk in peace with your boo.

We all realize that Prince Akeem and his bride-to-be Imani are fictional characters. However, I have found in my own marriage that it just makes my husband's toes curl when I do whatever he likes. This has taken some sacrifice on my part, but I have also found great delight and joy in doing specific things to please my big hunka burning love. Not only that, it has enriched our marriage and made it quite enjoyable.

Prayerfully, this information has helped you and becomes revelation in your life. I trust you will not only read it, but put it into practice. I believe that if you do, you too will find great delight and joy in pleasing your husband. So, why don't you give it a try? The next time your husband asks what would you like to do, set your own desires aside. Bow slightly at the waste with your hands out and say, "Whatever you like."

Questions

1. What is the phrase that Prince Akeem's bride-to-be kept saying to him?
2. Why is marriage not for the spiritually immature?
3. Do you purposefully dress to please your husband?
4. What is your husband's favorite meal?
5. When was the last time you prepared something for him because you knew he liked it?
6. When was the last time you watched a sporting event with your husband?
7. Are you withholding sex from your husband even though you know he likes it?
8. Do you wear cute undergarments and sleep wear for your husband?
9. Do you need to replace flannel sleepwear for something a little softer?
10. According to Romans 12:18 what should you do to promote peace with your husband?

Memory Verse: 1 Corinthians 7:34 (NKJV) There is a difference between a wife and a virgin. The unmarried woman cares about the things of the Lord, that she may be holy both in body and in spirit. But she who is married cares about the things of the world—how she may please her husband.

Chapter 6

Respect
Find Out What It Means to Him

As I was preparing to write this chapter, I began to reflect on what I had written thus far. Chapters two through five can really be summed up in one word—respect. I mean think about it. The *No Talking Zone*, not nagging, submission and giving hubby what he wants really shows him that you respect him. If I had to sum it all up I would say the number one way to treat your husband like a king is to show him unconditional respect.

So what is respect? Isn't it ironic that Aretha Franklin[5] sang a song about respect, but her song referred to a man showing the woman, "a little respect?" I did some research and discovered that this song was originally performed by Otis Redding[6] (some more trivia for you). In his version of the song, he was pleading for the woman to give the man the respect due him. Aretha Franklin gave the song its popularity and it climbed the charts in the 70's which fed into the whole feminist movement that was quite prevalent at that time.

Respect is very simply defined as to give someone honor, reverence and esteem. Aretha's song was the clarion call for the woman of the 70's because women felt that they deserved respect just like men. This is true, yet, what does the Word of God say in regards to this issue of respect? We need to find out what it says and live by that before we start telling our husbands to give us a little r-e-s-p-e-c-t.

Before we delve into what the Word says about respect, I want to define the antithesis of respect which is disrespect. This word means to be discourteous, dishonor or to be rude. It also means to treat someone with or to show contempt. Some synonyms for disrespect are dishonor, impoliteness and irreverence. Keep both of these definitions in mind as we look to see what God has to say on the matter.

Ephesians 5:21-33 is often referred to in marriage counsel, conferences, books and messages on marriage. The husband is commanded to love the wife and the wife is commanded to submit to her husband. I want to turn your attention to Ephesians 5:33 as it relates to how a woman should treat her husband. I am going to show you what it says in a few translations to make it unmistakably clear as to how God wants us as wives to treat our husbands.

- **King James** - Nevertheless let every one of you -- in particular so love his wife even as himself; and the wife see that she reverence her husband.
- **Bible in Basic English** - But do you, everyone, have love for his wife, even as for himself; and let the wife see that she has respect for her husband.
- **English Standard Version** - However, let each one of you love his wife as himself, and let the wife see that she respects her husband.
- **God's Word** - But every husband must love his wife as he loves himself, and wives should respect their husbands.
- **Good News** - But it also applies to you: every husband must love his wife as himself, and every wife must respect her husband.
- **The Living Bible** - So again I say, a man must love his wife as a part of himself; and the wife must see to it that she deeply respects her husband--obeying, praising, and honoring him.
- **New American Standard** - Nevertheless, each individual among you also is to love his own wife even as himself, and the wife must see to it that she respects her husband.
- **New International Version** - However, each one of you also must love his wife as he loves himself, and the wife must respect her husband.
- **New King James** - Nevertheless let each one of you in particular so love his own wife as himself, and let the wife see that she respects her husband.

- **New Living Translation** - So again I say, each man must love his wife as he loves himself, and the wife must respect her husband.
- **Message** - And this provides a good picture of how each husband is to treat his wife, loving himself in loving her, and how each wife is to honor her husband.
- **Amplified** - However, let each man of you [without exception] love his wife as [being in a sense] his very own self; and let the wife see that she respects and reverences her husband [that she notices him, regards him, honors him, prefers him, venerates, and esteems him; and that she defers to him, praises him, and loves and admires him exceedingly].

Wow! Did you count how many times "respect" is referred to in these verses? Let me give you a hint. The word "respect" is found in each of these translations. This is so powerful because God is letting us wives in on a little secret. Men want respect! I realize that your beloved king may act up sometimes, BUT you just read several translations of the same verse commanding you as a wife to respect your husband. This concept is made crystal clear from this one verse of scripture. Now that you have read it means that you are accountable, and let me just add that if you do not respect your husband from this point forward...need I say more?

I am so convinced (and you should be too) that the Word of God is the answer to everything in life, including your marriage! If you would just take the time to study this verse alone, it would turn your marriage around on a dime. However, the challenge for most wives with this verse is that they feel that this kind of respect is only due to the husband that is doing EVERYTHING right. Should I even begin to talk about the fact that wives expect their husbands to be perfect, when they themselves are far from it?

Please note that Ephesians 5:33 does not mention the action or non action of the husband. Why? Because God is teaching the woman to show consideration and appreciation to her husband whether he deserves it or not. God is teaching His daughters to let their husbands know that in spite of any shortcomings, "I believe in you." God is trying to teach you that your husband wants to know that he is your hero and the way you display that is by showing him honor, reverence, esteem, deference and veneration even if he has not done things right.

This is not a difficult task if you process this through the unconditional love the Father shows you in spite of your shortcomings. Your husband may not be walking on water, but are you making it hard for him to obey the scriptures? If this is an area where you are falling short, should God treat you the way you treat your husband when he doesn't pay the bills on time? Should God belittle, badger, and bad mouth you when you forget to spend time with Him? Have you considered for one moment that the reason why your husband is doing what he is doing is because of the way you have been treating him? Think about it, and when you are done, go show your husband some respect.

My favorite translation of this verse is the Amplified version. Let's read it again. It says, "However, let each man of you [without exception] love his wife as [being in a sense] his very own self; and let the wife see that she respects and reverences her husband [that she notices him, regards him, honors him, prefers him, venerates, and esteems him; and that she defers to him, praises him, and loves and admires him exceedingly]." The instructions for the wife are to, "see that she respects and reverences her husband." The way that this translates is that as a kingdom minded wife you must make it your business to notice, regard, honor, prefer, venerate, esteem, defer, praise, love and admire your husband exceedingly!

In order to be thorough, I am going to share with you an acronym for "respect" that the Lord gave me as I was gathering my thoughts for this chapter. Each letter will cover a simple concept that I believe if adhered to will show your husband that he really is king of his castle.

R is for Reverence. According to the Merriam-Webster's dictionary, it means honor or respect felt or shown: deference; especially profound adoring awed respect. The first word in this definition is "honor." One of the things that Romans 13:7 teaches that as believers we are to give honor to whom honor is due. That seems like a simple enough command, but many wives have trouble giving honor to their husband even though the Bible commands it. The funny thing is that these same wives don't have a problem honoring their parents, bosses or supervisors, but don't even consider their husband on the list of those important enough to honor. This shouldn't be so. The Bible commands the wife to see to it that she respect her husband and encapsulated in that respect is reverence.

E is for Esteem. This word simply means to regard something with worth or value. If something that we own has worth or value we take care of it. Not only do we take care of it, we take special care of it. Do you take special care of your husband? I'm sitting here with my husband and I just looked over at him and asked, "Do I take special care of you?" He said, "Yes." Before and after I asked him the question, I immediately began to do a self check to make sure that I take good care of my sweetie. At first, I began to feel bad because I saw areas where I fall short. Then, even as I was writing this, the Holy Spirit reminded me of several things that I do from my personal appearance, to what I cook and everything in between, with Robert in mind. That brought great comfort to my soul, but there is still room for improvement. Try doing an esteem evaluation on yourself and see how you measure up. If you fall short, make the mid-term corrections and go forward from there.

S and P are for Special Priority. I wanted to give these two together to give more certainty of their use. These words need not be defined when read together as *special priority*. When anything is given special priority, it is handled different than something that is not so important. When I think of something being handled with special priority, I think of a package being mailed. This special priority handling is even higher than first class because it has to be treated with extra care in case the contents are sensitive, delicate or fragile. To tell the truth, most men would not consider themselves delicate or fragile, but what honor it would show them if you were more sensitive to their needs and gave them special priority in public and in private.

E is for Endorse. This can be summed up by you asking yourself, "Self, do I have my husband's back?" Merriam-Webster defines this word to mean, to approve openly, express support or approval of publicly and definitely. Which also asks the question, "Do you have your husband's back?" The back in regards to the physical anatomy of the body provides stability and support for the rest of the body. If a person has back problems it can affect anything from raising the hands to walking down the street. So, practically speaking, the way you can endorse what your husband is doing is to show your support for what he is doing. If he is a pastor, usher, businessman or whatever, be sure that you let him know that what he is doing is important to you and he has your support.

C is for Consideration. This means to think about what others feel and be careful not to hurt them. It also means to be understanding. Early in 2011 my husband preached a message entitled, *Love Doesn't Do That*. In this message he taught that love is encapsulated in consideration. This is very beautifully depicted in a Bible commentary that I came across several years ago on 1 Corinthians 13.

His message went through a series of things that love doesn't do, He made reference to a commentary in that message and I want to share it with you. It says, "Love suffers long, having patience with imperfect people. Love is kind, active in doing good.

Love does not envy; since it is non possessive and noncompetitive, it actually wants other people to get ahead. Hence it does not parade itself. Love has a self effacing quality; it is not ostentatious. Love is not puffed up, treating others arrogantly; it does not behave rudely, but displays good manners and courtesy. Love does not seek its own, insisting on its own rights and demanding precedence; rather it is unselfish. Love is not provoked; it is not irritable or touchy, rough or hostile, but is graceful under pressure. Love thinks no evil; it does not keep account of wrongs done to it; instead erases resentments. Love does not rejoice in iniquity, finding satisfaction in the shortcomings of others and spreading an evil report; rather, it rejoices in truth, aggressively advertising the good. Love bears all things, defending and holding people up. Love believes the best about others, credits them with good intentions, and is not suspicious. Love hopes all things, never giving up on people, but affirming their future. Love endures all things, persevering and remaining loyal to the end."

Wasn't that good? I trust it was good enough to inspire you to show your consideration for your husband by loving him with this kind of love. One of the ways that I show consideration to my king is that I go out of my way to be sure that I don't do anything to hurt him because he is the love of my life and best friend. I don't want to do anything to cause him grief.

T is for Treasure. When I think of this word, it brings thoughts to mind of something that is highly valuable and is given special treatment, consideration and care. Now I must say again that as I was writing this portion of this book, a few times, I had to check to be sure that I am daily giving Robert special treatment, consideration and care. I was a little troubled about my estimation of myself as I said before, that this morning I took it to the Lord in prayer. The Holy Spirit comforted my heart and let me know that my husband was not displeased with me, but there was room for improvement. I said, "Yes, Lord," and immediately put some things into action.

I charge you to pause, ponder and pay attention to what it means to treasure your husband. Ask the Lord to see how you measure up and if necessary, make the mid-term corrections. Don't put off tomorrow what you can do today. Prepare your husband a special meal, give him a card letting him know how much you appreciate him or whatever it takes to express that he is a treasure to you.

I like what my friend Eva did for her husband on his 50th birthday. He is not a social network kind of guy, which totally eliminates texts, emails and Facebook. So she sent out an email on Facebook asking people to send David texts and emails to wish him a happy birthday. The response was overwhelming and her husband was truly blessed by this small act of kindness. It was a simple way that Eva showed David that he was a treasure to her.

Well, that covers my acronym for RESPECT. I believe that if you take the time out to reverence, esteem, give your husband special priority, endorse him, show him consideration and treasure him, he will not be lacking in feeling respected by you. This is just another way of saying that if you Ephesians 5:33 your husband exceedingly, he will know that beyond a shadow of a doubt that he is respected by his queen.

Questions

1. What is the number one way that you can treat your husband like a king?
2. According to the text, what is the antithesis of respect?
3. What are ways that a wife disrespects her husband?
4. What does unconditional respect mean to you?
5. Which is your favorite translation of Ephesians 5:33 and why?
6. What does the acronym R.E.S.P.E.C.T. stand for?
7. Are there any areas where you are falling short in showing your husband respect?
8. What did you do to make the corrections?
9. According the text what are some things that love doesn't do?
10. How can your husband know beyond a shadow of a doubt that you respect him?

Memory Verse: Ephesians 5:33 (AMP) However, let each man of you [without exception] love his wife as [being in a sense] his very own self; and let the wife see that she respects and reverences her husband [that she notices him, regards him, honors him, prefers him, venerates, and esteems him; and that she defers to him, praises him, and loves and admires him exceedingly].

Chapter 7

Blow His Mind!

D on't put your marriage on autopilot. The profundity of that command is much more far reaching that it appears. About a month ago my sister Tressa and I were talking about marriage. She was telling me of a co-worker who stated that her marriage ended in divorce after many years because they put their marriage on autopilot. They just allowed it to fly itself, so to speak instead of putting in the work necessary to keep things fresh and alive.

I began this chapter with that statement because I don't want you to put your marriage on autopilot. It is so easy to do, especially if both spouses have become accustomed to the same old routine. However, I am persuaded that if you do your part to blow his mind, there is nothing another woman will be able to do to touch what you do for your husband. Whatever she can do, your husband will know beyond a shadow of a doubt that you can do better if you establish a regular pattern in your marriage of blowing his mind!

To blow someone's mind means to completely astonish and flabbergast them. I like to think of it as something that will leave that person speechless. Now I don't know about you, but when I think of blowing someone's mind, the first person that comes to mind is my husband. That's the one I want to make feel so great that it makes him feel like he can fly or walk on water! I want to leave my husband singing this 1974 song by Barry White entitled *Can't Get Enough of Your Love*[7] to me, for me and about me!

How can I explain all the things I feel?
You've given me so much
Girl, you're so unreal
Still I keep loving you
More and more each time
Girl, what am I gonna do
Because you blow my mind.

Girl, can you hear your husband crooning that song for you? I can! I am persuaded that none of you reading this today want to suffer the ill effects of your marriage on autopilot. I am also persuaded that one sure fire way to keep your marriage from being set on autopilot is to blow his mind! So, let's look at some creative ways to get hubby to say, "Baby, I just can't get enough of your love!"

As we delve into this subject matter of blowing his mind, we are going to start with some lessons from unlikely instructors. I trust you won't be moved by this new teacher I am going to introduce to you. She is an expert and if you let her, she will help you today. I've learned a few things from her myself and I'm truly grateful for her teaching. She has equipped me to guard my marriage with vigor and vehemence so that I won't have any stuff from the other woman! Are you ready? Well, let me introduce you to the teacher for the hour. Her name is Ms. Seductress and her assistant Ms. Immoral.

Now wait just a minute! Before you pack up to leave class because Ms. Seductress and Ms. Immoral have messed with your man, hear what they have to say. They have some wisdom to share if you can get past who they are. If you let them, they can help you! So, calm yourself down, open up your heart to hear what the Spirit of the Lord is saying!

The lesson plan for Ms. Seductress comes from the book of Proverbs. As I was reading over these verses, I thought to myself, "If she can do these things to lure my husband away, then surely I can do these things to blow his mind, so that he will never want to go out and play." Therefore, I am going to go through these verses with you so you too can gain some wisdom and insight on this matter.

Proverbs 5:3 says, "For the lips of an immoral woman drip honey, and her mouth is smoother than oil." Look at how this verse reads in the Message Bible. "The lips of a seductive woman are oh so sweet; her soft words are oh so smooth." Okay, so now, let's flip the script and gain some understanding. It is obvious by the fact that many saved, married men have been caught in Ms. Seductress's trap of sweet, smooth words that men like sweet smooth words! What if you took the time out to tell your husband that he is the straw in your berries, the honey in your tea and the whipped cream on your hot chocolate? I'm telling you it will blow his mind and keep him close to hear further just how sweet he is to you!

The next verse in our lesson from Ms. Seductress is Proverbs 5:20 which says, "For why should you, my son, be enraptured by an immoral woman, and be embraced in the arms of a seductress?" Here we see the two key words in this verse are "enraptured and embraced." To enrapture means to fill with overwhelming delight. Another way of putting it is immeasurable delight or pleasure that cannot be measured, because it is so intense. Here we have again Ms. Immoral and Ms. Seductress blowing a man's mind by giving him immeasurable delight and weakening him with her soft embrace. Ladies, I can't count the times I have counseled married women who are too tired for love off the Richter scale and can't remember the last time they sweetly embraced their husband. Those same women get a little bothered when I ask how they would feel if the other woman did what they are unwilling to do. Time out for excuses. As wives, we need to learn the lessons from the uncircumcised Philistine chicks. Don't be too proud, immature or insecure to do what you know will please your husband.

The next verse in our lesson comes from Proverbs 6:24-25. It reads, "To keep you from the evil woman, from the flattering tongue of a seductress. Do not lust after her beauty in your heart, nor let her allure you with her eyelids." Okay, so far we have covered speech and touch. This passage of scripture deals with how Ms. Immoral and Ms. Seductress lure a man away with her beauty. I remember going through a phase in my life when I was depressed, discouraged and in despair most of the time. As a result, I didn't put much effort into how I looked. Did I tell you about this already? Well, anyhoo, I just didn't care about my appearance, nor did I give any thought to being attractive for no other reason than to please my boo. Not to mention I felt very insecure at the mention of Robert telling me about the chicks at work drooling over him.

Needless to say, one day I got a revelation, and let me tell you that I am so glad I did! Now, whenever I get dressed, no matter where I am going I want to daily present to my husband his beautiful Nubian queen. You should do the same too; even if you don't feel you measure up to the beauty of Miss America. Besides, everybody may not be a Mariah Carey, Janet Jackson or Halle Berry, but you can work with what you have and be your husband's personal beauty queen!

The final passage we are going to learn from today is found in Proverbs 7:13-18. It says, "So she caught him and kissed him; with an impudent face she said to him: I have peace offerings with me; today I have paid my vows. So I came out to meet you, diligently to seek your face, and I have found you. I have spread my bed with tapestry, colored coverings of Egyptian linen. I have perfumed my bed with myrrh, aloes, and cinnamon. Come, let us take our fill of love until morning; let us delight ourselves with love." Do you see Ms. Seductress and Ms. Immoral at work? She has kisses and peace offerings. She has come out to meet this man (hopefully not your man) and she is one persistent woman because she did not stop until she found him. Then she began to entice him with the preparations that she had made in her bedroom and urges him to come and make love to her all night long!

Based upon our previous lessons from these two teachers, do you know where I am going next? I now want to know when was the last time you enticed your husband with kisses, a sweet smelling bedroom and promises of making love to him until he passed out. For some wives, (surely not you) the mere suggestion of such a thing would be mind blowing! But let me ask you this. Wouldn't you rather be the one blowing your husband's mind instead of another woman? Certainly and unequivocally your answer is yes. So therefore, why not learn from today's instructors? Follow their pattern and be prepared to blow his mind!

As I bring this chapter to a close, I want to reiterate that if you don't blow your husband's mind, Ms. Seductress, Ms. Immoral and all the marriage destroying demons will attempt to do the same. The enemy doesn't play fair and he is out for keeps. This is an age old problem that Christian marriages are not exempt from. Therefore, let's just keep before us (yes, me too) the practical things that can be done to keep our husbands yearning for more.

Remember, blowing his mind is done by doing the unthinkable. Therefore, this week, why not try to pay special attention to your king. Make him your special project for a whole week and go out of your way to do something nice and sweet for him each day of the week. This can be done by serving him breakfast in bed (I'm going to try this one!), give him a massage, leave love notes in conspicuous places or perhaps you may want to try planning a mystery date.

The possibilities are endless, so be creative. The goal is to prevent your marriage from being set on autopilot. Let your creative juices flow and ravish him by filling him with the delight of your love. Instead of looking to be swept off your feet, sweep him off his and let him know that it is your pleasure to fulfill his pleasure. In essence my sisters, my friends, pull out all the stops and just blow your husband's mind!

Questions

1. According to the text, what does it mean to put your marriage on autopilot?
2. Why do couples put their marriage on autopilot?
3. What does it mean to blow someone's mind?
4. What is a sure fire way to keep your marriage from being set on autopilot?
5. Who are the teachers on the lessons on how to blow your husband's mind?
6. What scripture verses were referenced in this lesson?
7. Which one stood out to you and why?
8. What are some of the ways Ms. Seductress and Ms. Immoral have lured husbands away?
9. What are you going to do to keep them from wreaking havoc in your marriage?
10. What are you going to do with the information that was presented to you in this lesson?

Memory Verse: Proverbs 8:33-35 (KJV) Hear instruction, and be wise, and refuse it not. Blessed is the man that heareth me, watching daily at my gates, waiting at the posts of my doors. For whoso findeth me findeth life, and shall obtain favor of the LORD.

Chapter 8

A Polished Jewel

Years ago, I read a book entitled, *How To Stop The Other Woman From Stealing Your Husband* by Apostle Louis Greenup. I first read it when I was single, and later read it a few times when I was married. I had picked up a new copy that I had purchased at a women's conference and read it from cover to cover on the plane ride home. I tell you, by the time I landed; I was ready to jump Mr. Robert Poole's bones!

It was an incredible read and I learned how to keep Ms. Seductress and Ms. Immoral at bay from two statements made in this book. One I will cover in this chapter and the other I will cover in chapter nine. The statement from that book that pertains to this chapter is, "The other woman *always* looks good." I tell you when I read that it shook me to my core. That was probably the impetus that jolted me into getting my act together in regards to my appearance. I made those changes over fifteen years ago and I haven't looked back.

A polished jewel is one that has been cleaned and buffed to bring out its brilliance. I especially love it when I have just cleaned my wedding ring because it really sparkles and shines! When the sun catches it at a particular angle the light from the diamond bounces off of any object it touches. It's truly something to behold and I enjoy moving my hand around while riding in the car, as I watch the lights from my ring dance on the dashboard.

Being the light that dances on his dashboard is really quite simple. All you have to do is take the extra time to sparkle and shine for the sole purpose of catching his attention. You know like a real life sun catcher that mesmerizes all who look on it. Keep in mind, you cannot be a sun catcher to your husband if you always look like you just rolled out of bed or just finished cleaning the house. Fix yourself up by day and by night giving him something to behold every time he is in your presence. And, please, whatever you do, don't have your husband meet with some counselor and say, "Hi, my name is Bob and I married a gang banger."

Yes, I discovered this just days after we got married. My vision of loveliness was getting ready for bed one evening and she put on some flannel pants, a t-shirt and tied a red bandanna on her head backwards. You know, kind of like Aunt Jemima on the syrup bottle. I had to rub my eyes to be sure that I was seeing what I was seeing because I had no idea that she even owned clothes like this. She obviously was very comfortable in what she was going to bed in because the next thing I know, she was in the bed, under the covers and on her way to her first dream. I crawled in the bed next to her, pulling the comforter up to my neck. I folded my hands behind my head and stared at the ceiling for what seemed to be hours. I finally drifted off to sleep saying to myself, "I can't believe I married a gang banger."

Surely this is not your testimony, and you do not have anything in your daywear or nightwear that would connect you with a gang. Now I know that some of us need to wear a scarf at night to keep the hair together, but you have to make the adjustments to please your husband. I know many men don't want their wives going to bed with any head gear on. If this is your husband, then you need to get a satin pillow case and learn to sleep cute. Another option is to turn out the lights so he doesn't have to behold you with your hair tied up and as soon as you get up in the morning take the scarf off. Before you even go into his presence, smooth your hair down and give him something pleasant to behold.

Then there's the issue of flannel sleepwear! I know the flannel gown or pajama set is your favorite, but news flash ladies, husbands DO NOT like for their wives to sleep in flannel. Besides, if you would be honest with yourself, you'd have to admit that it's stiff and itchy. Not to mention the fact that there is *nothing* sexy about flannel.

See, what you need to do is invest in some funderwear. What in the world is *funderwear?* Well, I'm glad you asked. Funderwear is sexy sleep wear that I renamed "funderwear" because it is fun to wear! Get it? If you are a bit cold natured like me, you may have to make some modifications in your acquisition of your new funderwear. However, just like Walmart sells flannel, so does

Victoria's Secret sell soft, sexy sleepwear in pants with a cute little camisole top. I discovered this about six years ago or so when someone bought me a satin pajama set. It was cute. It was soft, but I didn't like it because when I sweat satin makes me cold. So, I went to Frederick's to make an exchange and to my surprise I found this wonderfully soft, black pajama pant set. I went home and tried it on for size and let me just say that the rest is history! Robert loved it and I was warm and sexy at the same time. What more could I ask for?

So what I'm saying here ladies is that you must daily and purposefully give your husband something to feast his eyes upon. And don't think that he is not looking because he is! So, when you are getting dressed in the morning headed for work, ask yourself, "Self, what would Big Daddy want to envision me in today?" As you are perusing through your drawer full of dainties, select something that you know would make his toes tingle. Then, as you are pulling together your outer garments, select something that you have heard him say, "Girl, you look so good in that outfit it makes me want to sop you up like a biscuit!" The finishing touches come with a cute hairdo, nice jewelry and perhaps a little make-up if that's your thing. Don't forget to spray on his favorite perfume that you know will completely and unequivocally take his breath away.

My sisters, when you step out of the house polished and shining, anyone who would dare to take a gander would know that you are well spoken for. It's time out for getting all dolled up to get someone else's attention. You are now the queen and the only one you want to be enthralled with you is your king. I know that before you were married, you dressed to catch; but now you've been caught, so let the king know that you aim to please from head to toe.

You may find it difficult to take the extra time to doll yourself up because you don't like the way that you look. So, let's talk about that a little bit. I remember years ago two things that helped me in regards to my physical appearance. First, it was shortly after Shekinah was born and I hated on the little pooch that I had acquired. I took my hands and grabbed my stomach trying to squish it away saying, "I hate my stomach." The Holy Spirit immediately responded by telling me that I really didn't "hate" my stomach because I had done nothing to change it. The other thing was when the first lady of the church I went to told the Lord that she did not like how she looked. His response to her was to change. I said all that to say that if you do not like how you look, then change.

The key to change is training not trying. Have you ever *tried* to lose weight before? How successful were you? Not very, I imagine. Why? Because, trying involves no commitment. When you train, however, you set some goals to exercise and change your diet. It's really that simple. I have had the opportunity to share with women across the country, the weight loss plan of the ages. It's plain. It's simple and anyone can do it. It's called the P.T.P. B. & E. plan. If you would just Push The Plate Back and Exercise, you will see those extra pounds melt off of you like butter. Keep in mind that the change doesn't come overnight, but if you stick to it you will see the results. Also keep in mind that I am not saying that you are to try to be a size zero. You just need to purpose in your heart to do what you need to do to polish your appearance for your husband, especially if he has dropped a few hints; of which I am not going to go into right now. You know what they are!

As I was about to close out this chapter, I realized that I didn't give you any scripture references that back up this concept of being a polished jewel. It would seem that this would be understood without saying, but for those of you who need a little spiritual insight; I will give it to you. Although it is evident throughout scripture that some things are not said, but they are displayed. However, I too am a woman of the Word and I want you to be able to know what the Word has to say about your physical appearance.

In Proverbs 31:30 it says, "Charm is deceitful and beauty is passing, but a woman who fears the LORD, she shall be praised." 1 Timothy 4:8 states, "For bodily exercise profiteth little: but godliness is profitable unto all things, having promise of the life that now is, and of that which is to come." These scriptures hold great truths and need to be adhered to. However, remember, the other woman is always looking good in order to steal the hearts of husbands from their wives. Therefore, it would behoove you to handle your business.

Esther 2:12 is where we find the account of the women being prepared to go before the king. They went through six months with oil and myrrh, six months of perfume and other preparations that accompanied beautifying women. Those women were silky smooth, smelling good and something to behold by the time they went through an entire year of beautifications and preparations. I'm sure that all of those young ladies were beautiful, but the king chose Esther because he like the way she *looked*. She was truly a polished jewel. Look at how Esther 2:17 reads in the Bible in Basic English. "And Esther was more pleasing to the king than all the women, and to his eyes she was fairer and fuller of grace than all the other virgins: so he put his crown on her head and made her queen in place of Vashti." This verse makes it clear that Esther was more pleasing and to his eyes, she *looked* the best.

As you know, men are visual by nature, so what they see is important to them. The king took one look at Esther and she blew his crown sideways with her beauty. It's safe to say that he was quite smitten by her appearance because there were several women who were presented to him that day, but Esther was the one who took his breath away.

Let me leave you with these final thoughts on your appearance. Charm is deceitful, and for any of us that have had children, that beautiful flat belly of yesteryear is now marked up with stretch marks, stretched skin and other scars. Therefore, confidence in outward beauty cannot be the glue that holds your marriage together because beauty is passing. However, there is a beauty that will never fade away. It is the hidden beauty in the heart of every woman who fears the Lord. So, the epitome of a polished jewel is an inward attitude of the heart which is displayed in the wisdom of a godly woman who does all she can to be beautiful for her king.

Questions

1. What about the other woman should make you want to look good for your husband?
2. What should be the sole purpose of you sparkling and shining for your husband?
3. Is your husband married to a gang banger?
4. What is funderwear?
5. What should you do if you don't like the way you look?
6. What is the key to change?
7. What is the weight loss program referred to in this chapter?
8. Are you willing to give it a try?
9. What attracted King Ahasherus to Esther? Give the scripture reference.
10. What is the epitome of a polished jewel?

Memory Verse: Proverbs 31:30 (NKJV) Charm is deceitful and beauty is passing, but a woman who fears the LORD, she shall be praised.

Chapter 9

Satiate Him in the Garden

The premise for this chapter comes from a revelation that the Lord gave me on Proverbs 27:7 which says, "The full soul loatheth an honeycomb; but to the hungry soul every bitter thing is sweet." The Amplified translation paves the way for the revelation that the Lord spoke to my heart on this verse. "He who is satiated [with sensual pleasures] loathes and treads underfoot a honeycomb, but to the hungry soul every bitter thing is sweet." The revelation of this verse is, "*If he's full at home, there be no need to roam.*" Glory!

Before I go to the implications of a satisfying sex life from this verse, I want you to first think in terms of food. Do you know how full you get from eating say, Thanksgiving dinner? After you have eaten all that turkey, dressing, mac and cheese, greens and candied yams followed by the peach cobbler, sweet potato pie, German chocolate cake and banana pudding, you feel like you are going to pop! On the ride home from the relatives, none of the fast food joints or food bill boards even fazes you, because you were completely full and satisfied from dinner. Now, all you can think of is getting home to sleep off all the food you just ate.

The flip of this is how your body feels when you are fasting. You turn the T.V. on to check the weather and there just so happens to be a food commercial on. That food looks so good it makes you want to lick the T.V. screen! Later that day, you need to go out and run some errands. This time, every fast food spot you pass smells like they are cooking the food in the parking lot! Then you start drooling contemplating breaking your fast at Burger King! The final straw is when you go into the grocery store to pick up a few non-food items that as you pass the vegetables in the produce section, you almost want to break off a couple stalks of asparagus to nibble on as you make your way to the health and beauty section. Am I the only one who has felt like this before?

Well, the wisdom given in Proverbs 27:7 is true. If you are full, you don't want to eat. If you are hungry, you will eat anything, even if it is something that you don't particularly like. Now, think of this in terms of being sexually satisfied or sexually starved. I believe the reason why many husbands, (including the Christian ones), cheat is because they are not sexually satisfied from their wives. In fact, not only are they not satisfied, but they are starving for some sexual fulfillment, which the wife has failed to provide.

So, here we go. You want to treat your husband like a king? A lot of times, many times, a husband feels like the king of the castle no matter what else is going on in the world when he is sexually satisfied from his wife. This is not some deep, difficult, diametrical notion to figure out. Men love sex! They love it even more now that they are married and in their mind able to fulfill all their sexual pleasures with their beloved wife. However, somewhere and somehow, the wives have either ignored their husbands need for sex or decided that because they don't want to do the shake and swirl then, hubby just isn't gonna get to shake and swirl! What in the world is up with that?

Sisters, you better wake up and smell the coffee brewing in the kitchen! We all know as women that we can go on and on like the little *Ever Ready Battery Bunny* without sex. This is not good and it is not God. It is also a known fact that among women. Sometimes sex is not at the top of the most important things to do list. However, let me bring to the forefront of your mind something that has helped me through the years.

Remember that book I told you about in the last chapter? It was *How To Stop The Other Woman From Stealing Your Husband.* I mentioned there were two things from that book that revolutionized my thinking in this area. The first one was that the other woman always looks good. The other one was, is and forever will be that the OTHER WOMAN IS NEVER TIRED! Not only is she never tired, she is ready, willing and able to give up the back pay for your man and won't even think twice about the fact that he is married. Some of these uncircumcised Philistine chicks are so bold that they may even know you, have eaten with you and consider you a friend. None of this matters to this wicked woman. She has only one goal in mind and that is to satiate your husband in the dark of the night fulfilling his every sexual pleasure. Then when she is all done, depending on what type of other woman she is, your husband may be using your children's college fund to pay her!

All this is happening while you are saying things like, "Jim always wants to have sex. All he ever thinks about is sex, Sex, SEX!" "I'm too tired to have sex. John doesn't care though. He will roll me over like a piece of meat just to get some. How inconsiderate is that?" Let me tell you what is inconsiderate. The fact that you know your husband is so sexually starved that he is about to bust and all you can say is, "Not now Jerry. I'm tired." Then without any conviction, you roll right over and go to sleep mad at him as if he has done something wrong.

The truth of the matter is that you are the one who is wrong. Do you read your Bible? It clearly says in 1 Corinthians 7:3-6 that, "Let the husband render unto the wife due benevolence: and likewise also the wife unto the husband. The wife hath not power of her own body, but the husband: and likewise also the husband hath not power of his own body, but the wife. Defraud ye not one the other, except it be with consent for a time, that ye may give your- selves to fasting and prayer; and come together -- again, that Satan tempt you not for your incontinency." Did you see what it says in verse four about your role as a wife? Verse five goes on to say, "defraud ye not one the other." In other words, don't withhold from your husband his due benevolence! Notice the wording in this passage of scripture is not a suggestion; but a command, so there- fore, to withhold sex from your husband is a sin! What? Oh yes it is! Don't believe me? Look at this same verse in some other transla- tions to persuade you of this truth.

- **Amplified** - The husband should give to his wife her conjugal rights (goodwill, kindness, and what is due her as his wife), and likewise the wife to her husband. For the wife does not have [exclusive] authority and control over her own body, but the husband [has his rights]; likewise also the husband does not have [exclusive] authority and control over his body, but the wife [has her rights]. Do not refuse and deprive and defraud each other [of your due marital rights], except perhaps by mutual consent for a time, so that you may devote yourselves unhindered to prayer. But afterwards resume marital relations, lest satan tempt you [to sin] through your lack of restraint of sexual desire.

- **Bible in Basic English** - Let the husband give to the wife what is right; and let the wife do the same to the husband. The wife has not power over her body, but the husband; and in the same way the husband has not power over his body, but the wife. Do not keep back from one another what is right, but only for a short time, and by agreement, so that you may give yourselves to prayer, and come together again; so that satan may not get the better of you through your loss of self-control.

- **English Standard Version** - The husband should give to his wife her conjugal rights, and likewise the wife to her husband. For the wife does not have authority over her own body, but the husband does. Likewise the husband does not have authority over his own body, but the wife does. Do not deprive one another, except perhaps by agreement for a limited time, that you may devote yourselves to prayer; but then come together again, so that satan may not tempt you because of your lack of self-control.

- **God's Word** - Husbands and wives should satisfy each other's sexual needs. A wife doesn't have authority over her own body, but her husband does. In the same way, a husband doesn't have authority over his own body, but his wife does. Don't withhold yourselves from each other unless you agree to do so for a set time to devote yourselves to prayer. Then you should get back together so that satan doesn't use your lack of self-control to tempt you.

- **Good News** - A man should fulfill his duty as a husband, and a woman should fulfill her duty as a wife, and each should satisfy the other's needs. A wife is not the master of her own body, but her husband is; in the same way a husband is not the master of his own body, but his wife is. Do not deny yourselves to each other, unless you first agree to do so for a while in order to spend your time in prayer; but then resume normal marital relations. In this way you will be kept from giving in to satan's temptation because of your lack of self-control.

- **King James** - Let the husband render unto the wife due benevolence: and likewise also the wife unto the husband. The wife hath not power of her own body, but the husband: and likewise also the husband hath not power of his own body, but the wife. Defraud ye not one the other, except it be with consent for a time, that ye may give yourselves to fasting and prayer; and come together again, that satan tempt you not for your incontinency.

- **The Living Bible** - The man should give his wife all that is her right as a married woman, and the wife should do the same for her husband: for a girl who marries no longer has full right to her own body, for her husband then has his rights to it too; and in the same way the husband no longer has full right to his own body, for it belongs also to his wife. So do not refuse these rights to each other. The only exception to this rule would be the agreement of both husband and wife to refrain from the rights of marriage for a limited time, so that they can give themselves more completely to prayer. Afterwards, they should come together again so that satan won't be able to tempt them because of their lack of self-control.

- **New American Standard** - The husband must fulfill his duty to his wife, and likewise also the wife to her husband. The wife does not have authority over her own body, but the husband does; and likewise also the husband does not have authority over his own body, but the wife does. Stop depriving one another, except by agreement for a time, so that you may devote yourselves to prayer, and come together again so that satan will not tempt you because of your lack of self-control.

- **New International Version** - The husband should fulfill his marital duty to his wife, and likewise the wife to her husband. The wife's body does not belong to her alone but also to her husband. In the same way, the husband's body does not belong to him alone but also to his wife. Do not deprive each other except by mutual consent and for a time, so that you may devote yourselves to prayer. Then come together again so that satan will not tempt you because of your lack of self-control.

- **New King James** - Let the husband render to his wife the affection due her, and likewise also the wife to her husband. The wife does not have authority over her own body, but the husband does. And likewise the husband does not have authority over his own body, but the wife does. Do not deprive one another except with consent for a time, that you may give yourselves to fasting and prayer; and come together again so that satan does not tempt you because of your lack of self-control.

- **New Living Translation** - The husband should fulfill his wife's sexual needs, and the wife should fulfill her husband's needs. The wife gives authority over her body to her husband, and the husband gives authority over his body to his wife. Do not deprive each other of sexual relations, unless you both agree to refrain from sexual intimacy for a limited time so you can give yourselves more completely to prayer. Afterward, you should come together again so that satan won't be able to tempt you because of your lack of self-control.

- **The Message** - The marriage bed must be a place of mutuality--the husband seeking to satisfy his wife, the wife seeking to satisfy her husband. Marriage is not a place to "stand up for your rights." Marriage is a decision to serve the other, whether in bed or out. Abstaining from sex is permissible for a period of time if you both agree to it, and if it's for the purposes of prayer and fasting--but only for such times. Then come back together again. Satan has an ingenious way of tempting us when we least expect it.

- **Wuest New Testament** - Let the husband be rendering to his wife that which is due her, and also let the wife render to her husband that which is due him. The wife does not have authority over her own body, but her husband does. Likewise also the husband does not have authority over his own body, but the wife does. Do not continue to rob each other [by withholding yourselves from one another] except it be by mutual consent for a time in order that you may give yourselves to prayer, and that you may be united again, in order that satan may not solicit you to sin because of your lack of self-control.

Did you pick up what the translations of this passage of scripture are putting down? It's in your Bible and the command is clear; you are not to refuse your husband sex. It's what is due to him as a husband and to you as a wife. At this point, I am not even talking to unsaved wives because they are not seeking the Lord for instruction and guidance in their marriage. I am talking to you, saved woman, who knows what the Word of God says concerning this matter, yet refuses to obey. Yes, I said it; refuses to obey. I can't even begin to count the women I have talked to who said they were too tired to have sex with their husband so they only did it a few times a month. I can't even begin to tell you of the wives that we have spoken to in marriage counsel who can't remember the last time they were intimate with their spouse. I can't even begin to tell you the countless number of women who really don't see that their withholding sex from their husband is a sin. I can't even begin to tell you because time would fail me and my computer would probably crash if I tried to put it all in this book.

This ought not to be so among the community of born-again believers. About fifteen years ago, I had some of the ladies over my house for fellowship. Somehow, as only ladies can do, we happened upon the subject of sex. I want to say there were maybe five of us there and out of the five, four of them agreed that they were too tired to have sex. I took that as to mean, since they were too tired, that they didn't do it very often.

Now, let me say that I was the only one that said that wasn't my testimony. Please don't take it as me bragging because I am not. My boast is in the Lord. He helped me to see through the women who were constantly and consistently trying to get with my husband that I had better call on Him for energy and strength! And, ladies, let me tell you that is exactly what I did. I told the Lord that I too suffered from being tired. He reminded me that the other woman is never tired and the same Spirit that raised Jesus from the dead was at work in my body giving me life! From that point on, I began to trust God to help me fulfill my husband's sexual needs. And, the truth of the matter, I had sexual needs too. I was just more tired than I wanted to have sex, so sleep would win all the time. God is no respecter of persons, so I know that if you pray and ask the Lord for strength, He will give it to you. Besides, you have no problem praying and asking God for new shoes, clothes and Coach purses. You have no problem praying and asking Him to heal your body, help your children and save your harassing neighbors. Why, oh why then won't you just pray and ask the Lord to give you strength in order to please your husband sexually? He said in 1 John 5:14-15 that if you ask Him anything according to His will He will hear you and He will grant you the petitions that you have asked of Him. You just read a plethora of translations that state that it is God's will for you to make love with your husband; so what are you waiting for? Turn your face to the wall and repent. Then ask Him for the strength to meet your husband's needs and expect an answer.

I failed to mention the meaning of the garden. I wanted to go ahead and interject it here to be sure to give a clear picture of what I mean when I say, "*Satiate him in the garden.*" We understand that when God created Adam and Eve, they were placed in the Garden of Eden; and they were naked and unashamed. Picture this. Since they were naked in the garden, everything they did, they did naked. They ate, slept, milled about, came and went in the garden naked. My husband and I use this to encourage husbands and wives to be intimate. We tell them to go home, find a baby sitter (if they have little ones) close the blinds, go to the garden and do everything naked. Just like Adam and Eve did everything naked in the garden we tell them to do the same and see what happens. "Just go to the garden," we say. "It will really revolutionize your marriage if you try this a few times a week or whenever is needed."

So, now that you understand that the garden is your love chamber, it is a shame that many wives have more excuses than the law allows as to why they don't go to the garden. The list of excuses is so long that if there was a dollar attached to every excuse, the money acquired would be enough to get somebody out of debt. This is just wrong! Not only is it wrong, this is something that should not even be named among Christians. I came across a book called *Intimacy Ignited*[9] by Dr. Joseph and Linda Dillow and Dr. Peter and Lorraine Pintus. There was a letter in that book adapted from Dr. Dillow's book, *Solomon on Sex*[10]. The letter in the book is funny, but sad at the same time. The letter reads:

To my dear wife,

During the past year I have tried to make love to you 365 times. I have succeeded only 36 times; this is an average of once every 10 days. The following is a list of why I did not succeed more often:

It will wake the children	17 times
It's too late	45 times
It's too early	23 times
Pretended to be asleep	18 times
Headache	23 times
Backache	9 times
Toothache	4 times
Too full	12 times
Giggles	2 times
Baby is crying	15 times
Company in the next room	8 times
Windows are open ("neighbors will hear")	9 times
You had to go to the bathroom	12 times
Gained weight ("don't touch my new cellulite")	6 times
Too hot	15 times
Too cold	7 times

There's a good movie on	15 times
Not in the mood	89 times
Total	329 times

During the thirty-six times I did succeed, the activity was not entirely satisfactory due to the following:

You chewed gum the whole time	6 times
You watched TV the whole time	5 times
You said, "Hurry up and get this over with."	17 times
You fell asleep	6 times
You never moved and I thought you were dead	2 times

Honey, it's no wonder I'm so irritable!
Your loving husband

Now that you've gotten a good laugh, would your husband write this same type of letter about you? If so woman of God, you should be ashamed of yourself. This is not the kind of letter that should be written of any Christian wife. However, I know some husbands who echo the sentiments of this poor, sexually frustrated husband.

I'm spending a little more time on this chapter hoping that you will allow the Lord to speak to your heart if you are being disrespectful, discouraging and downright stingy in the garden. The Bible is crystal clear on sexual matters and God doesn't bite His tongue so as to teach husbands and wives not to reject each other sexually. Sad to say, most of the rejecting comes from the wife. As you see from the list above, the reasons for holding out on her husband are quite elaborate and extensive.

As I said before, and you have read it for yourself in 1 Corinthians 7:5 that to withhold sex from your husband is a sin. It's a sin because God commanded you stop depriving one another of due benevolence, and if you are depriving your husband sex, then you are being disobedient to this verse of scripture. This is aside from the fact that although you can't stand Ms. Immoral and Ms. Seductress, every time you hold out on your husband you give her the keys to your house and welcome her into your sacred garden to get with your man. Surely that is not what you are trying to do.

There are a few other things that I want to point out from 1 Corinthians 7:5. First, the only reason couples should abstain from sex is if they both agree to it. Next, the only reason to abstain is for one and or both to pray and seek God on a matter. Finally, this period of abstinence should only last a few days because, prolonged periods of no sex in a marriage, opens the door for the enemy to come in and steal, kill and destroy everything that God had intended for that marriage.

What is the solution? Instead of withholding sex, satiate your husband in the garden! Put that brother on tilt so that when he comes out of the garden with you he can't see, speak or stand up straight. The husband is given some explicit instructions to be satisfied with the wife of his youth in Proverbs 5. Verses 18 and 19 say, "Let thy fountain be blessed: and rejoice with the wife of thy youth. Let her be as the loving hind and pleasant roe; let her breasts satisfy thee at all times; and be thou ravished always with her love." Let me show you this verse in a few other translations.

- **God's Word** - Let your own fountain be blessed, and enjoy the girl you married when you were young, a loving doe and a graceful deer. Always let her breasts satisfy you. Always be intoxicated with her love.
- **The Living Bible** - Be happy, yes, rejoice in the wife of your youth. Let her breasts and tender embrace satisfy you. Let her love alone fill you with delight.
- **New Living Translation** - Let your wife be a fountain of blessing for you. Rejoice in the wife of your youth. She is a loving deer, a graceful doe. Let her breasts satisfy you always. May you always be captivated by her love.
- **The Message** - Bless your fresh-flowing fountain! Enjoy the wife you married as a young man! Lovely as an angel, beautiful as a rose-- don't ever quit taking delight in her body. Never take her love for granted!

Pay attention to the last sentence in each of these translations. The husband is to be intoxicated with his wife's love. He is to let her love fill him with delight. He is to be captivated by her love and is to never take her love for granted. So yes, your husband has his instructions, but you have a part to play in the garden as well. In order for you to keep your man on tilt, you have a responsibility. It starts with you dying to yourself. Then you must ask the Lord to help you to be a servant lover and keep his love tank so full that the thought of going after another woman will be nauseating.

I opened this chapter with my revelation of Proverbs 27:7. Remember that I said, "If he's full at home there will be no need to roam." This can truly come to pass as you yield yourself to the Lord and seek to please your husband. If this is done, by you and your husband, you will both be so satisfied with each other that you will not desire to seek satisfaction elsewhere. Isn't that wonderful?

As I bring this chapter to a close, I want to bring this to your attention. Sex is a beautiful thing that God created for a husband and wife to find physical satisfaction and pleasure from one another. It is a tool that God has given to establish oneness between you and your king. However, I know that many wives (the saved ones too) use it as a weapon against their husband. Now I trust this is not you; but I know of wives who have sent their husband over to the couch ministry because of an argument. You do know what the couch ministry is right? It is the place where the husband is sent to when his wife is mad and says, "You ain't getting none tonight! Go sleep on the couch!" I have also heard of wives who manipulate their husband by saying things like, "If you want some, you better be sure to do what I asked you to do." "I'll take you to the garden if you take me shopping." "I don't know what makes you think we are doing that tonight. You were late home from work, again." These are all weapons that drive a wedge between a husband and wife and many times this wedge, if driven deep enough will send him right over to the other woman! Again, sex is a beautiful tool; so purpose in your heart to use it to the glory of God. Don't be tricked by the enemy into using it as a weapon. It may cost you your marriage.

Another thing that I want you to keep in mind as I close out this chapter is that these are not my instructions. I have shown you in the Word of God that these instructions come from the Lord. So, don't be shy. Satiate your king in the garden and let him know that you delight to fill him with your love. Keep your man on tilt! Intoxicate him with your love, so that no matter who may come trying to flirt with him, he won't even look their way because he is full to the brim of your love for him.

Questions

1. What was my revelation/translation of Proverbs 27:7? Did this help you and how?
2. What will make your husband feel like king of his castle?
3. How does the statement, "The other woman is never tired," affect you?
4. Should you deprive your husband of sex? Give scripture reference?
5. When is the only time you should deprive your husband of sex?
6. What should you do if you are too tired for sex?
7. According to the text what is "the garden?"
8. Instead of withholding sex from your husband what should you do?
9. Proverbs 5:19 says that your husband is to be intoxicated with your love. Are you making it hard for him to obey this scripture?
10. According to the text, what did God create sex for?

Memory verse: 1 Corinthians 7:3-6 (MSG) The marriage bed must be a place of mutuality--the husband seeking to satisfy his wife, the wife seeking to satisfy her husband. Marriage is not a place to "stand up for your rights." Marriage is a decision to serve the other, whether in bed or out. Abstaining from sex is permissible for a period of time if you both agree to it, and if it's for the purposes of prayer and fasting--but only for such times. Then come back together again. Satan has an ingenious way of tempting us when we least expect it.

Chapter 10

Always & Forever

Robert and I have been married now for 19 wonderful years. We decided when we got married that we would renew our vows every seven years. So far we have done it twice and both ceremonies were beautiful. Currently, I am in the process planning the third one that will take place on July 7, 2013, on some beach somewhere. I am really looking forward to that.

Anyway, when we did it five years ago, we had some friends sing our theme song which is "Always and Forever"[11] by Heatwave. Read the lyrics to this song.

Always and forever
Each moment with you
Is just like a dream to me
That somehow came true
And I know tomorrow
Will still be the same
Cause we've got a life of love

That won't ever change and…
Every day
Love me your own special way
Melt all my heart away
With a smile
Take time to tell me
You really care
And we'll share tomorrow together
I'll always love you Forever

There'll always be sunshine
When I look at you
It's something I can't explain
Just the things that you do
And if you get lonely
Phone me and take
A second to give to me
That magic you make and..

Every day
Love me your own special way
Melt all my heart away
With a smile
Take time to tell me
You really care
And we'll share tomorrow together
I'll always love you Forever

Whenever I hear this song my heart swells with love and adoration for Robert. Our lives together have truly been like a dream come true for the both of us. Right now, I am on a plane traveling home from Phoenix and I can't wait to see him so he can melt my heart away with his smile. He always takes time to tell me how much he really cares for me, and displays it even in the little things that he does. I look forward to spending the rest of my life with him, always and forever.

Prayerfully this is the type of affection you feel in your heart for your king. I have discovered on this journey called marriage that this type of romantic love is available for every couple who is first willing to submit to the Lordship of Jesus Christ. After that, things can't help but to fall into place because you are merely walking out your love for your husband out of obedience to the Lord.

This is why I started this book out wanting to show you the importance of you having a revelation of King Jesus. If he is first in your life, it will be easy to say, "Always and forever, it's you and me babe." However, for some I know this is easier said than done. Nevertheless, if Jesus is Lord, will you trust Him to make the crooked places straight and the rough places smooth in your character (yes I said your character), enabling you to treat your husband like the king that he is.

In order to keep this song burning in your heart, purpose to take the principles and precepts taught in this book and apply them to your life. Remember, you can do all things through Christ who daily infuses strength in you. Therefore you can stick and stay, respect and honor, love and cherish your husband whether he is acting like the king that he is or not. So really, your part has nothing to do with his action or non-action. It's all about being obedient and bringing honor to the Lord. The choice is yours.

I just left my friends, David and Eva in Phoenix. I love their marriage. They have been together now for 20 years and their love for one another is strong. While we were together, we talked about our spouses and she shared something with me that was profound. She said, "The early years of our marriage were hard. I could have gotten out and at one point, I told David that if he did not change I was out." He knew that she was not bluffing, so from that point forward their marriage turned around. After that, they still had to work through some things, but she decided that by the grace of God she would endure and did. God has changed them both and they are the better for it.

I wanted to share that because I know David and Eva personally. I can attest to the fact that their individual love for the Lord is the glue that has held their marriage together through the hard times. They are committed to the Lord first, so their commitment to one another is binding.

Remember Keeba that I talked about in chapter three? Well, she and her husband Jeff have been married now for over 11 years. Their marriage is a testimony to the transforming power of the Word of God. I asked Keeba what was the determining factor that changed their marriage around. She said, one day, they both went home and made a commitment to do the Word. She is no longer a contentious nag and goes out of her way to treat Jeff like a king.

What it all boils down to is choices. Eva and Keeba choose to obey God. Which will you do? I ask this because as I said before, marriage is not for the spiritually immature and you have to decide wholeheartedly by the grace of God that for better or worse, you will obey God. The romantic love is beautiful and available, but the truth of the matter is, that's the icing on the cake and if you got married to experience that on a day to day basis, you are (if not already) in for a crashing disappointment.

However, there is hope for all of us! If you do your part and treat your husband like a king with honor and respect, he will meet and fulfill your desires of romance, love and affection. He will go with you on walks in the park. He will take you to the beach so that the both of you can be captivated by the sunset. He will do all the romantic things for you and with you, just because he loves you. The key is you must do your part.

Well, glory! Our journey has come to a close and I trust that you have been tremendously blessed by this book. I have truly enjoyed writing it and I have been inspired to purpose in my heart to always treat Rob like a king. My prayer is that this book would bring deliverance, break yokes and cause you to overcome in your marriage.

Before I go, let me share with you in a little more detail my testimony. Prayerfully, it will inspire you to know that you can overcome and treat your husband like a king out of your attitude of gratitude for what the Lord has done for you.

As I look back over my life, I realize, recognize and know that God has been good to me in spite of me. You see, I was not always a good girl. But God, being rich in mercy, blessed me with an incredible husband. It is because of my friendship, relationship and partnership with Rob that I know my Redeemer lives! I have experienced first class mercy, and as a result, I have purposed in my heart, out of an attitude of gratitude, to treat my Robert like a king.

What every little girl needs is the love of her father. Both my parents were in the home when I grew up, and I know my dad loved me. However, the love he gave me was not enough; so I sought for it in relationships with boys at a very young age. I lost my virginity at 13 and unbeknownst to me, that totally opened the door for all kinds of demonic influence in my life. From that point on I was starving for love and found myself looking for it in all the wrong places.

I just wanted to be loved and I was desperate! I looked high and low, but in the end, my search was like grasping the wind and I always came up empty handed. It wasn't until my freshman year in college when I was spiritually bankrupt that I began to even consider looking to God. My search began when I cried out to God in the midst of my affliction of herpes. I will never forget that day lying in my dorm room bed wondering, "Why me? What did I ever do to hurt anyone?" All I wanted was for someone to love me for me.

I later came to find out, as many of you know, that the wages of sin is death. I was steeped in sin; therefore, I was suffering the consequences of my sin. There is no way around that and I have no one to blame for my condition except me. My mom had taught me better, yet I chose to go my own way. As my life was as low as it could have gotten, I realized that my mother was right all along.

I managed to escape my freshman year in college with my life and I was now looking for a fresh start. In the January of 1987, I went back to school at Arizona State University. Shortly after I got there, I prayed a prayer that changed my life forever. I said, "Lord if you are real, show me." That was it and I went on about my business. Well, God answered that prayer and on March 27, 1987. I gave my heart to the Lord. I had finally found what I was looking for: someone who would love me just for me. My life has never been the same since.

For further details of my story you can read my first self-published book entitled *He Redeemed My Time*. Glory to God, I've come to know by experience that my Redeemer lives! I know that my Redeemer lives because He completely changed and rearranged my life and I am forever grateful. I know that my Redeemer lives because in spite of me, He blessed me with my husband, king and boo Robert James Poole, Jr.

Through his tender love for me, I experience the love, grace and mercy of God. I don't deserve it, but Robert loves me anyway. I'm not always easy to get along with, but Robert loves me anyway. I have hormonal issues just like any other woman, but Robert loves me anyway. Every day I experience the love of God to an imperfect, undeserving woman through my husband and for that, I'm just grateful.

That's why I treat my husband like a king. I suffered from the "wanna be married blues" most of my single, saved life. I was quite persistent to find a husband, but God so graciously intervened. Knowing this, how could I disrespect, disregard or treat with disdain such a wonderful gift given to me by God? So, with everything in me and the help of the Holy Spirit, I purposely honor the gift that God has given me in my king.

Robert is such a wonderful man of God and I am honored that God chose me to serve beside him in the kingdom. I don't ever want to take his love for me for granted, that's why I make it my business to defer, honor, praise, regard, esteem, love and admire him exceedingly. That's what the Word of God says, so out of an attitude of gratitude, I obey God and treat Robert like a king.

All of us have a testimony; but unfortunately, all of them don't have a happy ending. You may be really struggling in your relationship with your husband and the thought of treating him like a king may be nauseating. However, my prayer for you is that the principles laid out before you in this book will give you a glimmer of hope. Purpose in your heart to apply these things I have shared with you and give them time to work in your marriage. Remember, all truth comes in seed form and it takes time for seeds to grow and bear fruit.

Well my sisters, and friends, this concludes our journey. Always and forever means just that: Always and Forever. As you purpose in your heart to always and forever submit to King Jesus, may He, by the power of His Holy Spirit, enable, empower and inspire you to always and forever, treat your husband like a KING.

About the Author

P astor Sheila D. Poole is a wife, mother, pastor, author and motivational speaker. She has a heart for the word of God and relies solely on the Word as it is the source of everything she needs in life. She has self-published two books entitled *He Redeemed My Time* and So, You *Want to Get Married? Let's Talk*! Both books have been a tremendous blessing to the body of Christ as she candidly shares from her life experiences to help strengthen and encourage believers. She has recently written two new books, *Words of Encouragement* and *Lamplight Devotional.*

She and her husband Pastor Robert Poole are the founding pastors of Destiny Christian Center in Las Vegas, Nevada where God has commissioned them to "Illuminate the pathway to purpose through the teaching of God's Word." In July of 2002, the Lord graced them to meet their Bishop, Apostle Nathaniel Holcomb of Christian House of Prayer in Copperas Cove, Texas. From that meeting, a covenant connection was made and as of October 26, 2003, Pastors Robert and Sheila Poole were officially ordained by Apostle Holcomb becoming a part of the Covenant Connections International family. In June 2007, she and her husband were a part of the first graduating class of Sonship School of the Firstborn at the Christian House of Prayer in Killeen, Texas. They started the

Sonship School of the Firstborn at Destiny in September of 2007 and as of June 2011, the school has 54 alumni. IT'S ALL ABOUT HIM!

They have been married for 19 years and through their tender love for one another, God has anointed them to minister very candidly to marriages. Over the past 8 years they have ministered at several marriage conferences encouraging couples to simply obey the word. The Lord has truly blessed their relationship, and Pastor Rob very powerfully fulfills Ephesians 5:25 by loving his wife as Christ loves the church daily giving his life for her. Pastor Sheila in turn makes it her business to defer, honor, praise, regard, esteem, love and admire him exceedingly. Through their union, God has blessed them with two beautiful, born-again children: Joshua and Shekinah.

Resources

Books by Pastor Sheila Poole

He Redeemed My Time

So, You Want to Get Married? Let's Talk!

Words of Encouragement

Lamplight Devotional

Treat Him Like a King

Books by Pastor Robert Poole

Treat Her Like a Lady

Soon to Come

The Secondary Wife

All available soon at www.hunterheartpublishing.com.

For more information about Destiny Christian Center, speaking engagements or if you would like to do a Making Your Marriage Marvelous Conference/Seminar/Retreat in your area, please contact us:

By mail: 800 North Bruce Street, Las Vegas, NV 89101
By e-mail: 4Hm4Life@gmail.com
By phone: 702-383-0777

We look forward to hearing from you soon!

Bibliography

Introduction

[1] Robert J. Poole, Jr.: Treat Her Like a Lady Copyright © 2011 Hunter Heart Publishing, DuPont, Washington.

Chapter 1

[2] Page 9: Rick Renner: Sparkling Gems From the Greek Copyright © 2003 Teach All Nations, a division of Rick Renner Ministries, Tulsa, Oklahoma.

Chapter 4

[3] Page 51: The English Standard Version Study Bible Commentary (Note on Genesis 3:16) Crossway Books, Wheaton, Illinois.

Chapter 5

[4] Page 59: Coming to America (John Landis, Produced by Leslie Belzberg, George Folsey and Jr. Mark Lipsky, Company - Distributed by Paramount Pictures, Copyright © 1988, USA.)

Chapter 6

[5] Page 75: Aretha Franklin: Respect (Produced by Jerry Wexler, Writer Otis Redding, Label Atlantic Records, Copyright©1967.)

[6] Otis Redding: Respect (Produced by Steve Cropper, Writer Otis Redding, Label Volt/Atco, Copyright ©1965.)

Chapter 7

[7] Page 88: Can't Get Enough of Your Love: Barry White (Produced by Barry White, Writer Barry White, Label 20th Century Records, Copyright ©1974)

Chapter 8

[8] Page 97: Apostle Louis Greenup: How To Stop The Other Woman From Stealing Your Husband Copyright © 1994 Kingdom Word Press, Battle Creek, Michigan.

Chapter 9

[9] Page 117: Joseph and Linda Dillow and Dr. Peter and Lorraine Pintus - The Letter: Intimacy Ignited Copyright © 2004 NavPress, Colorado Springs, Colorado.

[10] Page 117: Joseph C. Dillow: Solomon on Sex Copyright © 2004 NavPress, Colorado Springs, Colorado.

Chapter 10

[11] Page 125: Always and Forever: Heatwave (Produced by Barry Blue, Writer Rod Temperton, Label Epic Records, Copyright © 1977.)

Contact us:

Hunter Heart Publishing
P.O. Box 354
DuPont, Washington 98327

publisher@hunterheartpublishing.com

(253) 906-2160

www.hunterheartpublishing.com

"Offering God's Heart to a Dying World"